Cross-Cultural Communication
for the Tourism and Hospitality Industry

Cross-Cultural Communication

for the Tourism and Hospitality Industry

REVISED EDITION

Helen FitzGerald

Hospitality
Press

Copyright © Pearson Education Australia, 1998, 2002

Pearson Education Australia
Unit 4, Level 2
14 Aquatic Drive
Frenchs Forest NSW 2086

www.pearsoned.com.au

Publisher: David Cunningham
Copy Editor: Ross Gilham, Ginross Editorial Services
Proofreader: Ross Gilham, Ginross Editorial Services
Cover, design, and typeset by: Lauren Statham, Alice Graphics

Printed by Pearson Australia Demand Print Centre

1 2 3 4 5 06 05 04 03 02

National Library of Australia
Cataloguing-in-Publication Data

FitzGerald, Helen, 1940- .
    Cross-cultural communication for the tourism and hospitality industry.

    Rev. ed.
    Bibliography
    Includes index.
    ISBN 1 86250 514 4.

    1. Tourism—Australia. 2. Tourism—Employees—Training of—Australia.
    3. Intercultural communication. I. Title.

338.479194

 An imprint of Pearson Education Australia

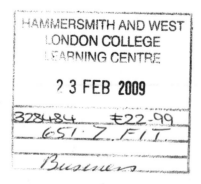

Contents

Acknowledgments

This textbook was compiled 'on the run' as the course entitled 'Cross-Cultural Communication' was being taught at Canberra Institue of Technology (CIT). Additions and modifications were made over a number of semesters. The information came from many sources including individuals with specific knowledge, personal first-hand experience, and a wide variety of written sources.

Two colleagues, in particular, contributed to the preparation of some of these materials, and I am most grateful for their input. Colleen Fox contributed to the early drafts of the sections on *Japanese*, *Indonesians* and *Germans*, and Margaret Byrne did the initial work on *Malaysians*. These two colleagues also contributed ideas for the *Questions* and *Answers* sections, and made a number of other suggestions which proved very helpful.

Gratitude is also extended to Margaret Wong for her helpful information on the preferences and needs of Chinese visitors.

I would also like to thank Pam Robertson, a Head of Department at CIT. This course is part of the *Advanced Certificate in Business Hospitality* offered by her department. Her agreement to trial a flexible mode of delivery (in which students familiarised themselves with these materials at their own pace, prior to a weekly class tutorial) made possible, during these tutorials, a variety of other activities and discussions based on some knowledge.

Sincere thanks are due to the editor, the Rev. Dr Ross Gilham, for his painstaking editing and reorganising of the text, and for his extensive additions to the chapter on *Religions and Philosophies* (in particular the section on *Christianity* which he contributed). He also provided the excellent *Index* and made substantial contributions to the Appendix *Facts & Figures*, and to the *Glossary*.

Thanks also to Professor Robin Jeffrey of La Trobe University for his advice on the text on *Hinduism* and *Indians*.

▼

The text of this book was submitted to the Australian Embassies (or High Commissions) of the following countries: Japan, Thailand, the United States, Singapore, Indonesia, the Republic of Korea, Germany, Malaysia and India. Sincere thanks are extended to the officers of the embassies for their helpful expert suggestions. The editorial input from the embassies has been very valuable in ensuring the accuracy and balance of the material presented, but the individual embassies are not responsible for the final text.

A Note on References

In general, references were not noted down (especially from newspaper and magazine articles) as this book was written, but details of the references included in the text, and a list of the main sources, are provided in the *Bibliography*.

H.F.
Canberra
September 1997

▼ Introduction

●●●

About This Book

This book has been designed to be used by personnel training for, or working in, the Tourism and Hospitality Industry. It can be used for self-study purposes, as preparation for class tutorials during a course, or for support materials for cross-cultural training courses.

The cultural groups chosen for inclusion represent:

▼ those which are important sources of overseas visitors to Australia (or growing markets); and
▼ those which have cultural values, communication-styles, behaviours, expectations and preferences which differ from those of most Australians.

Much of the information which is included would also be helpful for Australians working overseas or in multicultural workplaces in Australia.

According to a report of the Office of Multicultural Affairs, *Productive Diversity in the Tourism Industry,* the greatest economic growth in the future is expected to be not from the main historical foreign language markets of Japan and Europe, but from the nearby Asian markets composed of Chinese (several dialects), Korean, Indonesian/Malay and Thai speakers. This report recommends increased research into the specific needs of such visitors. The report also notes that the Australian tourism industry employs substantial numbers of people from non-English-speaking backgrounds, especially in the hospitality sector.

Although the material in this book is written from an Australian point of view, it has also been used with many international students, usually from Asia, who have found it of value in learning about Asian cultures other than their own, and also in learning more about mainstream Australian culture by the comparisons made (either explicitly or by inference). Their helpful comments, appreciation and enthusiasm have been of great value.

The course begins with a section on *Important Religions and Philosophies*. This is certainly not intended to be a theological textbook containing great detail on each religion or philosophy. It aims to give only a general overview of the subject, with information which will be of assistance to staff and students in the hospitality industry. A 'working knowledge' of this material will be an invaluable introduction to the subject, before proceeding to discuss individual cultural groups.

Following this introduction to important religions and philosophies, the book presents a series of sections on *various cultural groups* of importance to the Australian tourism industry. Each section on a given cultural group is complete in itself, and the different sections could be studied in any order, or a selection made as required.

Following these notes on various cultural groups, sections follow incorporating *Questions* and an *Answers Guide*. There is a separate set of questions and suggested answers for each cultural group. The aim of these Question and Answer sections is to check comprehension and to reiterate key points, thus aiding retention of these points. Although specific answers must necessarily be given, students are encouraged to form and express opinions of their own about the points raised, and their thoughts on the implications for the hospitality industry. The Answers Guide section is therefore provided primarily for students working on their own, or for teachers new to the subject matter.

A comprehensive *Glossary* is included to assist with technical terms. This Glossary has been compiled with the aim of assisting not only the general readers of this book, but also those whose first language is not English. This feature will be of special assistance to those teachers whose classes contain students from countries other than Australia.

Whilst on this subject of teaching the course, teachers will find a section entitled *Teachers' Notes* in Appendix I at the end of this book. These notes contain:

▼ some thoughts on introducing the subject to students for whom the concept is new;

▼ the use of the Question and Answers sections as the basis for possible case studies; and

▼ the place of 'role-plays' in the teaching of a course such as this.

Appendix II follows, and this contains some useful *'Facts and Figures'* on the tourism industry in Australia.

A *Bibliography* and an *Index* complete the book.

Rationale for Cross-Cultural Communication Studies

There are strong arguments for cross-cultural communication studies for all those involved in the tourism industry, including managers, decision makers and those who have direct contact with people from other cultures. These contacts could reasonably be described as 'crucial encounters' which have the capacity to make or break the industry. Communication, culture and service are inseparable.

We are all culture-bound. Our culture is so much a part of us that we are not aware of its influence. Our own ways of behaving and thinking can seem right, natural and normal, and it is easy to forget that they are very much the result of our own cultural conditioning (that is, what our parents, schools and society have taught us directly or indirectly).

The biggest problems in cross-cultural contacts arise when people lose sight of this 'cultural conditioning' and tend to think of their own cultural attitudes as being universally shared and as part of basic human nature. They then assume that others are just like them and have the same ideas of what constitutes polite, acceptable behaviour. They take it for granted that other people have the same needs and expectations. Studying other cultures helps individuals to overcome resistance to the idea of difference, a resistance which is often a result of a simple lack of awareness of how others think and feel.

The reality is that visitors from other cultures arrive with behaviour patterns, expectations, needs and preferences based on their very different cultural conditioning. The quality of a service can then be measured only by how well it meets the visitors' expectations and needs. If service is to cater for both the domestic and international markets, it has to be very flexible to meet such diverse needs.

When receiving international visitors, the challenge is to retain the unique identity of the host culture while at the same time being able to put ourselves in the position of our guests, thus ensuring that they are satisfied, rather than made to feel embarrassed or uncomfortable.

Business and government now accept the need for such training in many areas, and universities are offering general cross-cultural communication courses.

▼

Cross-cultural training for staff pays off. To give only two examples cited in Shames and Glovers' *World Class Service* (1989):

▼ After such training was introduced at the New York Sheraton in 1984, the Japanese clientele grew by 250 per cent in two years.

▼ In 1981, the *Scandinavian Airlines System*, a travel company with a hotel chain, was on the verge of losing US$20 million. One year later it was earning in excess of US$24 million. A major part of the changes introduced in 1981 was to set the goal of meeting customers' expectations and, preferably, surpassing them. One way it achieved this goal was by introducing cross-cultural training.

General Perceptions of Australia

This book is written primarily for those working or training in Australia, with a view to helping them better serve overseas visitors to Australia. The book will therefore necessarily focus on Australian perceptions of foreigners. However, to do so, Australians need to be aware of how foreigners might perceive Australia.

Australia, in general, lacks 'status' as a tourist destination, because it is often perceived to be an 'empty' country populated by kangaroos and other exotic wildlife. It is important that Australians be aware that this will be the 'starting point' for many overseas visitors. The cosmopolitan and rich cultural nature of Australia needs to be promoted to the potential overseas tourist market.

Australians should also be aware of Asian sensibilities regarding Australia. The Asian press has a tendency to highlight any news emanating from Australia which suggests that Australia is critical or intolerant of Asian culture and political life. This may or may not be a fair representation of Australian attitudes, but it is a fact of life of which the Australian tourist industry (and those who work in it) must be aware. Political and diplomatic controversies in Australia inevitably influence Asian perceptions of Australia.

The Problems in Making Generalisations

There is a dilemma which is inherent in writing a book such as this. The whole purpose of the book is to encourage understanding and acceptance of the cultural traditions of others. Such an aim clearly stands in opposition to any notions of prejudice. However, as soon as an author tries to say anything meaningful about ethnic groups, traditions or cultures, generalisations become necessary. Indeed it is virtually impossible to say anything worthwhile about cross-cultural training without making such generalisations; and herein lies the dilemma. Immediately a generalisation is put forward, there will undoubtedly be 'exceptions to the rule', and there will always be someone who can say that the author lacks sensitivity and subtlety in making such a generalisation. It is easy to label a generalisation as being a 'stereotype'. With the best will in the world, it is impossible to completely avoid this dilemma. Generalisations are a 'necessary evil' in a book such as this.

The author can only appeal to the generosity of the reader in asking for understanding of the dilemma, and acceptance of the fact that the overall aim of this book is most certainly to decrease insensitive prejudice, and not to promote it.

The author is very much aware that generalisations about cultural groups, however carefully worded, will be modified by such factors as:

▼ regional differences within the group under consideration;
▼ religious differences within the group under consideration;
▼ educational differences within the group under consideration;
▼ economic differences within the group under consideration;
▼ the effects of 'modernisation' and 'Westernisation' (especially the influence of modern mass-communications and international travel); and, of course,
▼ the fact that individuals remain individuals in even the most 'collectivist' of societies, and individual persons must always be met and respected as persons in their own right.

The author is aware of all these factors, and everything written in this book should be read with an appreciation that the author is sensitive to all these matters.

Having said that, differences do exist between various cultural groups, and the members of any particular group do share common beliefs, customs and traditions which are different from those of other groups. If the author is to say anything meaningful about any group of people, generalisations are inevitable. It is the profound hope of the author that this book will promote empathy, understanding and tolerance of the rich cultural traditions which characterise humanity.

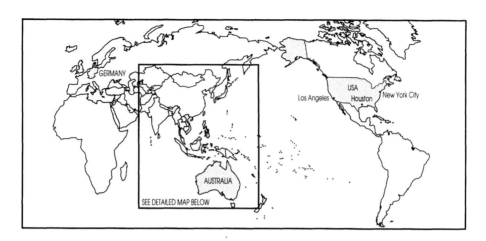

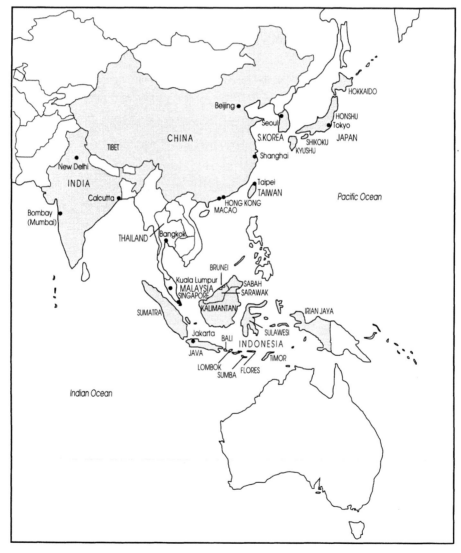

Important Religions and Philosophies

•••

The following is a very brief outline of the important religions and philosophies of most visitors to Australia. It would be helpful to read this section at the outset of the course as some knowledge of these religions and philosophies helps when studying the different groups that are influenced by these beliefs.

A book such as this cannot give detailed descriptions of complicated and controversial subjects like religion and philosophy. The descriptions which follow are not intended to describe these various religions in the sort of detail which might be found in theological textbooks. What we are interested in here, is to give a broad outline of each religion/philosophy to help students in the hospitality/tourism industry (or people interested in business dealings with overseas visitors) to better understand people from different cultures. If you are interested in exploring these issues in greater detail and subtlety, please consult the many textbooks on these complex and sensitive topics.

Islam

A major world religion

Islam is a major world religion. It began as a result of the teachings of Allah as conveyed by the prophet Muhammad (spelt in various ways in English) in Arabia in the 7th century CE (the 7th century of the Christian Era). It then spread rapidly from Africa and Europe to Asia, including Indo-China and Indonesia.

Although exact statistics are not available, the Muslim world population is estimated at more than 935 million. Islam has flourished in very diverse parts of the world. The major ethnic groups composing the Islamic world include the Arabs (North Africa and the Middle East); Turks and Turkic peoples (Turkey, parts of the former USSR, and Central Asia); Iranians; Afghans; the Indo-Muslims (Pakistan, India, and Bangladesh); South-East Asians (Malaysia, Indonesia, and the Philippines); and a small percentage of Chinese. In Europe, Islam is the second largest religion after Christianity.

Allah and Muhammad

The followers of Islam are called Muslims. According to Islam there is no God but Allah, and Muhammad is the messenger of Allah. The word *Islam* means submission to the will of Allah and complete obedience to his laws. Another way of expressing this is to say that Islam means conforming one's own will to the will of God. The events of life are seen as ultimately reflecting the will of Allah, with less emphasis being placed on the idea of events' being the result of individual human effort. Although Muslims do have choice in life, the will of Allah is paramount. Like Christians, Muslim theologians debate the idea of 'pre-destination' (the idea that the fate of an individual is decided by God from the beginning).

The main beliefs of Islam lie within the same tradition as Judaism and early Christianity. Muslims believe that Muhammad was the last in a line of prophets beginning with Abraham, and including Moses and Jesus. Like Christians, they believe in a heaven (paradise) and a hell.

The Koran and the Hadith

According to Islam, the will of Allah is made known through the Koran (or *Qur'an*). This is the holy book of Islam and Muslims believe that it records the actual words of Allah as spoken to Muhammad. The Koran is thus said to be infallible (that is, to contain the exact word of God and therefore to be without any error whatsoever).

The *Hadith* contain the sayings of Muhammad and information about him. They were compiled from the accounts of followers who lived at the same time. Unlike the Koran, which was memorised (in whole or in part) by many followers of Muhammad during their lifetimes, and which was written down quite early, the transmission of Hadith was largely oral, and the present authoritative collections date from sometime later (in the 9th century CE).

Therefore, unlike the Koran, Hadith is not considered infallible. Because Hadith was mainly transmitted orally, it is generally conceded that error could have entered into the tradition as it was passed down from generation to generation. Hadith, therefore, is secondary to the Koran, although it is almost equally essential for most Muslims.

Islam and social life

Islam regulates the total relationship of the individual to Allah, and lays down rules for behaviour in relation to the social, economic and political aspects of life. The holy writings of the Koran and the Hadith dictate strict rules for social matters such as inheritance, marriage and divorce. They stress the equality of all Muslims.

An area of particular sensitivity involves the treatment of women. In general, Islam preaches respect for women. However, there is legal discrimination and unequal treatment of women in some Islamic societies who believe that the Koran requires it. Others would dispute this view and claim that such treatment is not actually based on the Koran.

The major sects of Islam

Two major sects of Islam emerged after the death of Muhammad. They are known as the *Sunni* and the *Shi'ite* (or *Shia*). Muhammad made no provision for a successor, and his followers quarrelled among themselves. This resulted in two often hostile sects, a situation which continues until the present day.

The overwhelming majority of Muslims throughout the world are Sunni, including those in South-East Asia, which is one of the main areas of interest to this book.

Shiites are in the majority in Iran, and large numbers of Shiites are also found in Iraq, Syria, Lebanon, India, Pakistan and parts of Central Asia. Their total number is approximately 80 million (out of approximately 935 million Muslims worldwide).

The pillars of Islam

For observant Muslims, religion is a part of their daily life. The Muslim legal and social codes set out guidelines for every kind of decision. The basic objective is to prepare for the Day of Judgment by leading a just and ethical life. This involves meeting the obligations of the five 'pillars' of the religion:

▼ swearing allegiance to Islam (Allah and his messenger Muhammad);
▼ praying five times each day facing Mecca;
▼ making at least one pilgrimage (*hajj*) to Mecca;
▼ giving a certain amount to charity; and
▼ fasting during the month of Ramadan.

Dietary and other restrictions

Islamic dietary laws are spelled out in the Koran. Their purpose was to establish a sense of social identity and separateness from others, specifically Muslims from Jews. Many of these laws are similar to the Mosaic laws of the Jewish Old Testament. Muslims are forbidden to eat blood, the flesh of pigs, and the flesh of animals that are found dead. Muslims should eat only *halal* meat (that is, meat which has been slaughtered according to Islamic ritual requirements). The Koran also condemns and forbids drinking any intoxicating beverages. Gambling, moneylending and earning interest on money are also forbidden.

Ramadan

During the month of Ramadan, all Muslims must fast from sunrise to sunset, and abstain from other practices such as smoking and sexual intercourse. At the end of this month they celebrate the *Eid ul-Fitr* festival. This is an important festival to give thanks to Allah and to celebrate the end of Ramadan. Since Ramadan occurs in a lunar cycle (and not according to a calendar year), the month occurs at different times from year to year.

Christianity

A major world religion

Christianity is based on the life and teachings of a Jewish prophet known as Jesus of Nazareth, or Jesus Christ (which means 'Jesus the Messiah'). Christianity is the most widely distributed of the world religions, having substantial numbers of followers in all the populated areas of the globe. Its total membership exceeds 1.7 billion people. For the purposes of this book, Christianity has been especially important in the Western world (by which is usually meant Europe, North America, Australia and New Zealand). Christianity has been so important in the development of Western society that all of history is divided (according to the Western system) into the years before the birth of Christ (BC, before Christ) and the years after his birth (AD, or *annus domini*, 'Year of the Lord').

Jesus Christ

Jesus Christ was born in Bethlehem, a small village just south of Jerusalem. He had a relatively short teaching ministry of about three years during which he angered the Jewish religious authorities by preaching that love and forgiveness are more important in religious life than rules and regulations. He called God 'Abba' ('Father') and claimed to have an especially close relationship with God which allowed him to speak with authority on behalf of God.

Jesus taught that it was urgently important that the Jewish people listen to his gospel ('good news'), and many of his followers appear to have believed that the 'end of the world' was about to occur.

After a number of disputes with the religious leaders of the day, he was put on trial by both the Jewish and Roman authorities (who ruled Palestine in those times) and was executed by crucifixion (being nailed to a large cross and allowed to die by exhaustion and suffocation). The sign of the Cross has traditionally been the most important symbol of Christianity.

The followers of Jesus claimed that, after his death, he was seen alive on several occasions. This is known as the 'resurrection' of Jesus Christ, and is a central belief of Christian faith, symbolising the triumph of life over death.

As a result of his life and teachings, his followers believed that Jesus was more than merely a prophet or messenger from God. They said that he was the 'Son of God', or 'God in human form', and that his life represented God's decisive involvement in human history.

The New Testament and the Holy Bible

The teachings and actions of Jesus were recorded on the basis of accounts by his followers in a number of books called the New Testament. They record a large number of sayings of Jesus and also describe many 'miracles' (apparently supernatural events) concerning Jesus.

Christians also recognise the Jewish religious books (scriptures) as being holy books. These are called the Old Testament by Christians. The Old and New Testaments, taken together, are called the Holy Bible. Many Christians regard the Bible as being literally correct in every detail, and revere it as being the actual recorded Word of God. Others regard it as a holy book which is to be understood and interpreted as a collection of very important religious statements without being literally correct in detail.

The Eucharist

The most important part of worship for most Christians is the Eucharist (pronounced *'you-ka-rist'*), also known as the 'Mass' or 'Lord's Supper' or 'Holy Communion'. This involves the sharing of small portions of bread and wine which have been 'consecrated' (especially blessed) by a Christian priest or minister. This important ritual commemorates the last meal (or 'Last Supper') which Jesus shared with his followers before his death.

Christians believe that in sharing this commemorative meal together they are gathering in the presence of Jesus himself, although there is dispute amongst Christians about what the 'presence' of Christ actually means when they share this holy bread and wine. The Eucharist is especially important in the Catholic and Orthodox traditions, but is less important to Protestants (see below).

The Church and divisions in Christianity

The organised Christian religion (or 'Church') spread from its roots in Palestine to become the official religion of the Roman world, and from there it became the dominant religion of Western civilisation (including Europe and western Asia) for the next 2,000 years.

There have been two major divisions in the Christian Church.

The first division occurred in the 11th century ad when the western Catholic (meaning 'universal') Church split from the eastern Orthodox (meaning 'right-believing') Church. The division was based on complicated arguments about doctrine and authority, and continues to this day.

The second great split occurred in the western (Catholic) Church in the 16th century AD. This was known as the Protestant Reformation, and caused the western Church to be split into the continuing Catholic tradition, and the new Protestant group. This division has also continued until the present day. Moreover, the various Protestant groups have also split many times within themselves.

Catholics and Protestants in Australia

Despite considerable differences among themselves in doctrine and practice, Protestants generally agree in rejecting the authority of the Roman Catholic Pope, and in emphasising instead the authority of the Bible and the importance of individual faith. The term 'Protestant work ethic' comes from this emphasis on an individual's personal relationship with God, and personal responsibility for one's success in life. On the other hand, the Catholic tradi-

tion emphasises the importance of relationship with God through the established Catholic Church and membership of the shared community or 'Body
of Christ', with less importance being placed on the individual's personal
relationship with God.

In Australia the largest single denomination is now the Roman Catholic
Church. There are numerous smaller Protestant groupings. The Anglican
Church (until recently the largest denomination of Christians in Australia,
but now the second largest, after Roman Catholics) is sometimes described as
a 'middle way' between Roman Catholicism and Protestantism, and the
Anglican Church contains some members who would see themselves as
'Catholic' in their views, and others who would see themselves as definitely
being 'Protestants'.

Easter and Christmas

The most important events in the Christian calendar are Easter and
Christmas. Easter is a three-day commemoration of the crucifixion and resurrection of Jesus. It follows a lunar cycle, and therefore does not have a regular calendar date (although it always occurs sometime between late March
and late April each year).

Christmas is a celebration of the birth of Jesus and, in the Western tradition, is always celebrated on 25 December each year, although preparations
for the celebrations are now tending to begin several weeks before that date.

Christianity and the hospitality industry

There are no particular 'food laws' in Christianity, although some Christians
(especially Catholics) still observe the ancient tradition of avoiding red meat
on Fridays (as a mark of respect for the day on which the blood of Jesus was
shed on the Cross). Fish is still commonly offered on Fridays in Western
restaurants and hotels.

At Easter, chocolate eggs (representing 'new birth', or the resurrection of
Jesus) are traditionally exchanged and eaten. 'Hot cross buns' (a type of
sweet bread roll marked with a cross) are also eaten as a symbol of the crucifixion of Jesus on the Cross.

At Christmas time it is traditional to exchange gifts (often in association
with a decorated 'Christmas tree') and to share a large family feast, usually a
hot roast dinner (with turkey being the traditional meat). In modern times,
hotels and restaurants are increasingly popular as a venue for these big
family Christmas feasts.

▼

A turkey roast dinner is also part of the American tradition of 'Thanksgiving Day'. This important national day is discussed in the section of this book on *Americans*.

Some very devout Christians also observe self-imposed abstinence from pleasurable food and drink (and perhaps some other activities) during the weeks leading up to Easter and Christmas. These periods of time are called 'Lent' and 'Advent' respectively.

Some Christians (usually Protestants) do not drink any alcohol at all, and believe that it is sinful to do so (because of their emphasis on individual virtuous living). Most Christians (especially Catholics) are comfortable about drinking alcohol because Jesus appears to have shared bread and wine with his friends (see 'Eucharist').

Hinduism

The Hindus

The name Hinduism refers to the 4,000-year-old civilisation of the Hindus, a civilisation which had its beginnings in the Indus River Valley in north-western India (now Pakistan).

It is estimated that there are about 700 million Hindus in the world today, the vast majority being in India.

A religion and a philosophy

Hinduism is probably the oldest of the major world religions, taking shape from about 1500 BC (before Christ, or before the Christian Era). It is difficult to separate the religion from the cultural practices linked with this religion. Overall, it is a code of conduct as well as a body of beliefs, philosophies and worship practices. Hinduism has no real creed, organisation or founder. It contains many apparently contradictory beliefs and practices, and accepts all other religions as fundamentally true. A Hindu can believe in a non-Hindu religion as well as in Hinduism, and still remain a Hindu. The essential spirit is one of tolerance: 'live and let live'.

Sacred texts of Hinduism

The earliest sacred texts of Hinduism are the four *Vedas*. The oldest of the Vedas is the *Rig-Veda*, which was composed in north-western India between about 1300 BC and 1000 BC. It consists essentially of a thousand hymns to a number of gods. It has been carefully memorised and preserved orally to the present day. However, the best-known of the sacred Hindu texts is the *Bhagavad Gita* which is a profound philosophical poem explaining the duties of a Hindu. It is found in the great epic called the *Mahabharata*. The other great Hindu epic is the *Ramayana*. The two epics were gradually developed, but had largely been composed by about 100 CE. The most important gods of modern Hinduism—Shiva and Vishnu, Krishna and Rama—are found in the epics, but are not found, or are insignificant, in the much older Vedas.

The concept of *Brahman*

According to Hinduism there is a fundamental or ultimate level of reality (*Brahman*). It is the inner being and energising force of everyday existence. This belief is the basis of Hinduism, and also influenced the development of the other great Indian religions of Jainism and Buddhism. Existence at this deepest level is boundless. For example, time, space and the number of gods and goddesses are endless. Hindus believe that all possibilities can co-exist.

Reincarnation

Hindus believe in the transmigration of souls ('reincarnation'). Individual souls pass through a sequence of bodies or life cycles over an immensely long period of time. Achieving freedom from this cycle of birth, death and rebirth (*samsara*) depends on one's *karma* which is the consequence of all one's thoughts and physical actions. Each individual is fully responsible for his/her position in the next life or incarnation. Bad actions or thoughts result in bad karma, and a return to life in a lower position or non-human form. Good thoughts and actions result in good karma and a higher incarnation.

Castes

A feature of Indian life from time immemorial has been caste—a division of society into separate groups into which people are born. Each hereditary group (or caste) had inherited privileges or disadvantages. Much of traditional Hindu religious teaching is concerned with the duty of the individual to follow the rules, and fulfil the obligations, of the caste into which he or she is born.

The ancient Hindu texts divide society into four *varnas*, a word which can be translated as 'castes' or 'orders'. The first of these castes were the *Brahmins* who were the priests or moral leaders. The second caste were the *Kshatriyas* who were the warriors and administrators. Next came the *Vaishyas* who were the farmers, artisans and business classes, and fourth were the *Shudras,* who were peasants and craftsmen.

There was a group even below the Shudras, a group which had no caste. These people were 'Untouchables' because high-caste people were held to have been polluted if they touched them. The Untouchables performed the most menial and degrading jobs.

Except that Brahmins perform the priestly functions, the four varnas or traditional castes have had little relevance in Indian society or religion. In practice there are hundreds, even thousands, of separate castes or *jatis,* each with its own particular duties, customs and status. They can only theoretically be classified into one or other of the four traditional varnas.

However, the division between the caste Hindus and the Untouchables was, and remains, a real one. To this day the Untouchables (now called *Harijans* or *Dalits*) suffer grave social and religious disadvantages and perform the most menial tasks.

Caste is a most sensitive subject in modern India, and the position of the Untouchables is particularly sensitive. Discrimination based on caste is now against the law, but in practice it continues in spite of government efforts to prevent it.

Because it has been so fundamental to the structure of Hindu society caste is discussed further in the chapter on *Indians* later in this book.

The Hindu aims of life

The four aims of life are:

▼ the avoidance of pain and misery;
▼ worldly success;
▼ the faithful performance of one's duty; and
▼ eventual release from this life cycle.

Worldly success is seen as a social achievement, and has good implications for one's family, relatives, caste-group and society. Pleasure is regulated. One should limit sexual activity to one's spouse, and drugs and intoxicating beverages are sinful because of the harm they do. The final aim of Hindus (*moksha*) is the eventual release from this life-cycle. Then it is possible to merge with Brahman: the ultimate reality and the ultimate joy.

Hinduism outlines in detail all the duties that go with different stages of life, social status, sex and caste. Fulfilling the first three aims of life is a preparation for the ultimate aim. If people observe *dharma,* the law of right-living, they achieve the double objective of happiness on earth and moksha.

Dharma is the underlying order of the universe. Adhering to it contributes to harmony and cohesiveness in society. It sets down rules about personal habits, family and social ties, religious rituals and fasting. It also provides regulations about personal hygiene and food preparation.

Food and Hinduism

Food is an important part of Hindu life. Food is graded according to a system of purity/pollution. Cow's milk is ritually pure. Meats are graded according to their degree of pollution. Eggs are the least impure, and beef is the most impure. However, the highest caste (Brahmins) should completely avoid all meat products, and many other Hindus are also vegetarians. Orthodox Brahmins also avoid some strong foods (such as garlic and onions), and most Brahmins do not drink alcohol. This is not because it is polluting but because of the value Brahmins place on self-control. In some parts of India, the sale of alcohol is prohibited.

Buddhism

A pan-Asian religion and philosophy

Buddhism is a pan-Asian religion and philosophy. It has played a central role in the spiritual, cultural and social life of the Eastern world. It originated in India but spread to Sri Lanka, China, Tibet, Indo-China, Japan, Korea and other parts of Asia, whereas it declined in India. In each country, it took on new forms in response to local cultures, especially ideas of social stratification.

Many values and beliefs which are widespread in most Asian societies can be traced to the influence of Buddhism. Examples include the avoidance of conflict, non-assertiveness, humility, modesty, sensitivity to others, and the acceptance of silent suffering. Although many of these qualities are also taught in other religions (notably Christianity), they are especially prominent in Buddhism.

Buddhism and tolerance

An outstanding characteristic of Buddhism is its tolerance of other religions and philosophies. It allows belief in other faiths as well as in Buddhism. In general it has stressed the equality of people. However, in countries such as India, Japan and Korea, it supported the idea of a hereditary group of untouchables who were considered to be 'polluted' because their ancestors butchered animals.

▼

The founder of Buddhism

Siddhartha Gautama founded Buddhism. He was a prince who lived in the 5th and 6th centuries BC (before Christ, or before the Christian Era) in what today is northern India and southern Nepal.

Siddhartha was born into the tradition which we now call Hinduism, of the Kshatriya caste, but he rejected this religion as he did not agree with the ideas of the Brahmin priests. He wanted to find a way to end suffering and the seemingly endless cycle of birth and rebirth that also concerned Hinduism. After a long search, he achieved enlightenment through meditation and in this way became a *Buddha* (Enlightened One). He is the Buddha for our world now. There have been other Buddhas before, and more to come. The tradition of Siddhartha tells of the gods begging him to reveal how he had achieved enlightenment, and he spent the rest of his life preaching his ideas.

The teachings of the Buddha

Siddhartha taught that life is full of suffering and sorrow; that our experience of life is not permanent and is often unsatisfactory. The causes of this situation are craving, desire and ignorance. The only way to overcome suffering and earthly desires is to follow an eightfold path of training and disciplined morality. The aim is to reach the ideal state of *nirvana* (happiness or bliss). This is a condition beyond the limits of the mind, free of all material and earthly desires. People who are successful in doing this are freed from the cycle of birth and rebirth.

Sacred writings

The sayings of the Buddha were passed down orally for many generations, and the development of sacred writings was a piecemeal process which continued for centuries. No definitive sacred text exists (in the sense that Jewish, Christian and Islamic traditions, for example, have definite holy texts), but there are a number of writings which various branches of Buddhism believe to be of special and valued importance.

Numbers and divisions in Buddhism

The number of Buddhists worldwide is difficult to estimate, but is between 150 and 300 million. The explanation for this rather wide range of estimate is that throughout much of Asia religious affiliation has tended to be non-exclusive (that is, people can claim to be followers of both Buddhism and other religions simultaneously) and the exact number of Buddhists is therefore difficult to ascertain. The other reason for such a wide estimate is that the exact number of Buddhists in communist countries, such as China, is unknown.

Buddhism today is divided into two major branches known to their respective followers as *Theravada* ('the Way of the Elders') and *Mahayana* ('the Great Vehicle'). Theravada (also known as *Hinayana*, or 'Lesser Vehicle') has been dominant in Sri Lanka, Thailand, Cambodia, Burma and Laos, whereas Mahayana has had its greatest impact in China, Japan, Taiwan, Tibet, Nepal, Mongolia, Korea and Vietnam.

The 'rules of life'

Buddhism is moderate and does not advocate a life of strict abstinence. From the beginning Buddhism offered a Middle View or Path (*Madhyamika*). It is opposed equally to the extremes of denial and indulgence. This Path leads to enlightenment and eventually to nirvana, although many reincarnations might be necessary to achieve this. There are five rules of conduct. These are not strict prohibitions, but are more like desirable 'rules of training' which are undertaken voluntarily. These 'rules' are:

▼   undertaking not to harm any living things;
▼   abstaining from false speech (including gossip and slander);
▼   abstaining from taking what is not given freely;
▼   abstaining from sexual misconduct (including no sexual activity at all for monks, no marital infidelity for those with a partner, and no promiscuity for single people); and
▼   refraining from drugs or drink which cloud the mind.

Vegetarianism and Buddhism

The only 'food laws' of Buddhism which are relevant to the hospitality industry concern the question of Buddhism and vegetarianism. Many Buddhists are vegetarians because the killing of animals is prohibited. This prohibition of killing animals is actually stronger than the rule against eating animals.

Confucianism

Confucius and his philosophy

Confucianism was founded by the Chinese philosopher Confucius (K'ung-tsu) who was born in 551 BC (before Christ, or before the Christian Era). He and his disciples developed the Confucian philosophy. It focusses on human

▼

beings and society rather than on God and nature, and it rejects all supernaturalism. Since it has very few rituals and no concept of a god, it is more a moral philosophy than a religion. Nevertheless, there are thousands of Confucian temples and it has been regarded as a religion by some people.

For two thousand years the Confucian code was ideally the norm according to which all Chinese led their lives. This is still true for many Chinese.

The widespread influence of Confucianism

The influence of Confucianism has not been confined to China. Nearby countries such as Japan, Vietnam and Korea have also been strongly influenced by this philosophy and code of ethics, and are often described as Confucian societies. The predominantly Chinese societies of Taiwan, Singapore and Hong Kong are also strongly influenced by Confucian ideas. Because of its tolerance of other faiths, Confucianism developed alongside existing religions and was influenced by them, especially Buddhism and Taoism (now often spelt as 'Daoism' in English, to better reflect the Chinese pronunciation of the word).

The concept of Tao

The concept of Tao (or 'Dao') is central to Confucianism, and is basic to all systems of Chinese philosophy (not only Taoism). Tao ('heaven' or 'the Mandate of Heaven') is the ultimate principle underlying the universe. It is not transcendental or mystical, but has a moral quality and belongs to this world. Individuals cultivate themselves to achieve Tao. Then they use their talents and virtues to help others achieve Tao. The aim is that Tao may prevail in the world. Tao can also be translated as 'the Way'.

Confucian values

In Confucian doctrine a high value is placed on the collective, particularly the extended family, and on the predominant need for social harmony and the fulfilment of obligations to others. It is an hierarchical view of society in which the younger defer to the older, and women to men. It stresses filial piety: the importance of respecting and caring for one's parents. It teaches that virtue can be attained only through learning, and that anyone can rise to the top of society through education. As a result, all Confucian societies place great value on education. Other important Confucian values are: respect for age; obedience to authority; hard work; thrift; and the preservation of the good name of the family.

Economic growth and Confucianism

Some analysts have explained the recent economic successes of Confucian societies (such as Japan, Korea, Hong Kong, Singapore and Taiwan) as being due to the stress placed on collective effort, hard work and education. It is true that Confucianism, in general, encourages both individual achievement and the order and discipline that results from subjecting individual freedom to the greater good of family and society.

Taoism

Beginnings and influence

Taoism (now often spelt as 'Daoism' in English to better reflect the Chinese pronunciation of the word) is said to have been founded by the sage Lao-tzu who lived in about 500 BC (before Christ, or before the Christian Era). The essential Taoist philosophical and mystical beliefs can be found in the *Tao-te Ching* ('Classic of the Way and Its Power'), a text dating from about the 3rd century BC and attributed to the historical figure Lao-tzu although there is some debate about whether Lao-tzu actually wrote the book because of the discrepancy in dates between his life and the commonly accepted dating of the scripture.

The other important text in Taoism is the *Chuang-tzu*, a book of parables and allegories also dating from the 3rd century BC but attributed to the philosopher Chuang-tzu.

Together with Buddhism and Confucianism, Taoism is one of the major spiritual 'ways' of China, and, like Buddhism and Confucianism, it has also influenced Chinese thought in every aspect of life.

Taoist religion and philosophy

There are differences between the Taoist religion and the Taoist philosophy.

The Taoist religion is characterised by popular superstitions and magic, and promises physical immortality in return for faith. In this quest for immortality, Taoists use breath control, herbalism, dietary rules and techniques of sexual union.

The Taoist philosophy offers a form of nature mysticism and focusses on living naturally and simply in accordance with the Tao or Way. In this way, a person increases (rather than wastes) his/her vital, natural force. People who pursue fame and fortune are wasting these forces. They will be unable to conform to the natural forces of life, and thus be unable to achieve true holiness.

▼

Taoist influence on life-style

To simplify a complex subject, whereas Confucianism urged the individual to conform to the rules of an ideal socety, Taoism taught that the individual should ignore the dictates of society and seek to live only in accordance with the underlying pattern of the universe.

Taoism has a tendency to urge followers to avoid conflict and to conceal negative emotions. It represents the more carefree, joyful side of the Chinese character. At the philosophical level it is concerned with the bigger questions of the nature of reality. In this way it contrasts with the more duty-conscious and practical Confucianist philosophy.

It has been humourously observed that most Chinese are Confucian when things are going well for them, and Taoist when things are going badly!

Both Taoists and Confucians believe in the need for an harmonious balance in all things: for example, the strong, intellectual, assertive male (the *yin*) balanced by the gentle, intuitive, passive female (the *yang*). Taoist religion and philosophy are part of all cultures influenced by China, especially those of Japan, Korea and Vietnam.

Shintoism

Shintoism and nature

The word *Shinto* is Japanese for 'the way of the gods'. It is a Japanese cult and religion which originated in prehistoric times. During its early period, it was a body of religious belief and practice without a name, and it had no fixed dogma, moral rules or sacred writings. It worshipped a vast array of spirits, or *kami*, which represented various aspects of the natural world, including the sky, the earth, heavenly bodies and storms. (This form of nature religion is technically called an 'animist' religion.)

Shintoism today continues to retain characteristics of its early animist form with numerous shrines dedicated to nature spirits, dead heroes and other deities ('gods'). Shintoism stresses harmony between human beings and nature.

Shintoism and Japanese life

Shinto was the original religion of Japan, and Japan is the only country that follows this religion. Shintoism provides a mythological explanation for the founding of Japan, and the belief that the Emperor is divine.

In the 5th and 6th centuries AD (the 5th and 6th centuries of the Christian Era) Shintoism was strongly influenced by Confucianism, from which it adopted ancestor worship, and by Buddhism, from which it borrowed many beliefs and rites.

From 1868 until the end of the Second World War, it was the state religion of Japan, and the emperor was worshipped as a god (a belief no longer officially held in Japan).

Shintoism continues to be concerned with rituals rather than doctrines, and is closely interwoven with the social structure of Japanese life.

Japanese

Cultural Values

Japan today

Japan is a constitutional monarchy in eastern Asia, comprising four large islands, as well as more than 7,000 lesser adjacent islands.

In the Japanese language, the country's name is *Nihon* or *Nippon* ('origin of the sun'). From this comes the well-known designation of Japan as the 'Land of the Rising Sun'.

The population of Japan is approximately 125 million. Japan is an industrialised urban society, and the proportion of the population in the Tokyo, Osaka and Nagoya area now exceeds 43 per cent of the total population.

Japanese is the official language. In addition to speaking the official language, many Japanese also know some English.

Japan is one of Australia's most important tourist markets. However, there are some problems and Australia is in danger of losing its popularity. Problems include the following:

▼ Australia is seen as too expensive (it is cheaper for Japanese to visit Los Angeles);

▼ Japanese are unhappy about the insistence on visas for short-term visitors; and

▼ the lack of variety in accommodation is also sometimes criticised.

Because of these problems, the number of repeat visitors to Australia from Japan is about half the number who return for a repeat visit to Hawaii.

Australia's overall share of the total Japanese overseas tourist market is very small.

Most Japanese continue to travel in groups although Australia's popularity among independent travellers is rapidly developing.

An homogeneous society

Japanese policy is to assert that it is an ethnically homogeneous society. There are very strict immigration and citizenship rules to maintain this. However, apart from the ethnic Japanese who are in the overwhelming majority, there are small minority groups including Koreans, Chinese, the original inhabitants (known as the *Ainu*), and a group of 'untouchables' (or *Burakumin*). Despite government efforts, this last group is discriminated against because their ancestors allegedly engaged in 'unclean' occupations such as killing animals.

Religious faiths in Japan

A majority of Japanese say they have no religious faith. Most do not visit places of worship often. However, many have an altar in their home where they pay their respects on a more frequent basis. They follow the beliefs and practices of different religions and philosophies including Shintoism, Buddhism, Christianity and Confucian philosophy. People turn to different religions for various needs and life events.

Shintoism contributes to Japanese society an ideal of loyalty to one's clan, group or company.

Buddhism contributes an ideal of mentorship in the master/disciple model of Zen Buddhism, and also stresses the need for frugality, silent meditation and formality.

Confucianism contributes an emphasis on harmony and obligations to others.

Christianity is practised on a relatively small scale in Japan compared with the Eastern religions. However, at Christmas-time, commercial decorations and Christmas carols are evident in Japanese cities.

A society of rapid change

Within the span of a single lifetime, the Japanese have seen their homeland transformed from a mainly agrarian economy to an industrial economy, have then seen that industry destroyed by war, and have since seen their country emerge as a great industrial and economic power. Although the Japanese 'economic miracle' has run into some difficulties in more recent years, Japan is still a very prosperous nation.

However, despite these momentous changes, they have retained much of their traditional culture.

Japan now has the highest life expectancy in the world, and this is causing changes in society. Before industrialisation, men lived an average of only three years after retirement. Because of increased life expectancy, Japanese society is 'ageing' faster than other societies (that is, the percentage of the population classed as 'elderly' is greater than in most societies). There is a relative shortage of young male workers and, as a result, women are rapidly entering the workforce. More than 60 per cent of women now work, but seldom in top jobs. Many have part-time jobs with low pay and none of the good conditions usually associated with employment in large Japanese companies. They are the first to be retrenched in times of recession. Nevertheless, many young single women earn enough to travel. Working men are more tied to their jobs and have fewer opportunities to travel.

A 'collectivist' culture

Japan can be described as a 'collectivist' culture because there is more emphasis on group loyalty and interdependence (for example, the extended family, work colleagues and old classmates) than on fulfilment of individual desires and goals. Personal status and self-esteem is usually gained from the groups to which one belongs.

Japanese working men are expected to spend a lot of time socialising with workmates and building up good relationships.

The need for harmonious relationships (with no open disagreement) is a constant theme in the media and in workplace training. An important concept is the distinction between *honne* and *tatemae*. The former refers to truth (or the substance of a matter), and the latter refers to the public or official position. Japanese will avoid voicing honne in order to maintain harmony, especially in *soto* encounters (that is, encounters with outsiders). They are more likely to reveal their true feelings in *uchi* interactions (that is, with members of their 'in-groups').

Although it is possible to place exaggerated stress on collectivism and hierarchy in Japanese society, these values are, nevertheless, much more important than is the case in Australia. Children are generally trained (at home and at school) to value dependence, to be group-orientated, and to be aware of the status of others in relation to themselves. In the past the eldest son lived with his parents after marriage. Today, because of industrialisation

Gateway to Shinto temple at Miyajima, Honshu, Japan

and the move to cities, this applies to only about 15 per cent of households. However, the eldest son is still expected to look after his aged parents and take over responsibilities as the head of the family.

An hierarchical society

Japan tends to be an hierarchical society rather than an egalitarian one. Status is gained from gender, position, wealth and seniority. However, old age alone does not guarantee status as it does in some other Asian cultures.

In general, Japan is a male-dominated society. The Confucian teaching that a woman should obey her father in youth, and her husband in maturity, is widely followed. Women do not have social and economic equality, and almost all housework is done by women. However, women do have a lot of authority inside the home. For example, the family budget is usually controlled by women, and the husband often given a daily allowance. It is of interest (especially to the hospitality industry) that women generally decide where the family will go for holidays.

Arranged marriages now account for a minority of marriages, and the divorce rate is comparable with some Western societies.

Education is valued

Education is highly valued, and is tough and competitive from the beginning (when the race to get into the top universities begins at an early age). Most big companies choose new employees from these universities. Once at university, everyone passes examinations, and a job is virtually assured, so the time is spent building up important social connections.

A society of 'fads and fashions'

Japan is a society of mass 'fads and fashions'. It is important to be aware of this. In the 1980s, Canada became a fashionable holiday destination, but the Canadians were not ready to meet the needs and expectations of the Japanese. Consequently, the fad of travelling to Canada passed, Canada became less fashionable, and the Japanese tourist market to Canada collapsed.

Language and Communication

Verbal Communication

Language differences can present problems

Japanese tend to believe it is very difficult for foreigners to learn their language. They are therefore very appreciative and complimentary if others speak even a few words of Japanese.

Most Japanese now study English in secondary school. However, because of their examination system, they concentrate on reading and writing. They may thus have great trouble understanding spoken English (and an Australian accent), and may also have difficulty speaking English.

It is best to avoid negative questions such as:

▼ 'Didn't you get your key?'; or
▼ 'You're not leaving today, are you?'

In English, agreement is made by saying 'No'. However, because of Japanese grammar, Japanese will agree by saying 'Yes'. This is also true of many other language groups. It can be confusing for both sides.

Names and titles

Japanese are generally more formal than Australians. It is best to call them 'Sir' or 'Madam' or 'Mr' and 'Mrs', followed by surname. The Japanese style is surname followed by the word '*San*'.

The family name precedes the given name, for example, Mishima Yukio. However, in European languages, this is usually reversed for convenience.

Indirectness and silences are valued

Japanese communication-style is indirect: people are expected to guess what other people mean and what they want. Japanese believe that only an insensitive, uncouth person needs a direct and complete verbal message. Good communication is when the meaning is sensed without being explicitly stated. The ability to anticipate another person's message intuitively (the concept of *sassuru*) is highly valued. It is seen as a sign of maturity. The basis of this is a set of cultural values that emphasises *omoiyari* (which means 'empathy' or 'imagining oneself to be in another person's position').

People do not usually say directly what they want or think. *Enryo* ('reserve') is one of the most important values in Japan. It discourages people from expressing their opinions, desires or preferences. The Japanese language helps people to be indirect and not explicit. In Japanese the verb (the word naming the action) comes at the end of the sentence, and can be negated at the very end; for example,: 'Waiter this food customer give not'. In addition, any word which the speaker thinks the listener will guess, can be omitted.

It is polite to refuse an offer (for example, of food) two or three times before accepting. The host is expected to realise that the guest is actually hungry, and is merely showing enryo. Hosts should try to know the needs and preferences of their guests. Japanese in the United States have reported that it can be exhausting to be continually asked what they would like.

There is a proverb in Japanese: 'A man of many words has little refinement'. Japanese are used to pauses and silences during a conversation, and people who say what they really think and feel are seen as shallow and insincere. Generally, there is little obligation to make conversation unless one has something specific to say. When a senior man is present, he has the right to initiate speech.

Harmony is valued

The open expression of disagreement and anger is avoided. People try to 'sound-out' others and reach agreement. As with many other Asian cultures, 'face' (personal prestige) is very important to Japanese (much more than is the case in Western cultures). This means that people must avoid saying or doing anything that might make another person feel upset or uncomfortable; that is, cause them to lose 'face'. This is especially true of someone with higher status. The aim is harmony, with no direct criticism or unpleasantness.

For the same reason, Japanese try not to directly refuse a request. In this way they avoid hurting the feelings of others. They might agree very doubtfully, or even say nothing. In Japanese, there are many expressions such as 'Yes, well it's difficult', or 'I'll consider it', which normally mean a refusal. Children are trained in this style by their mothers. Japanese mothers do not say *'I* want you to do this'. Instead they say *'other people* will think your behaviour is shameful or strange', and they train their children to guess what other people are thinking or feeling.

A formal hierarchical system is accepted

Japanese use different names/titles/words to talk to (or about) other people, depending on whether or not they are members of their close group, and of the same gender/age/social status. It is very difficult for two Japanese to talk to one another until they know these things. This is one reason business cards are so important. It is also why it is not impolite to ask questions about age and income that might seem rude in English-speaking cultures.

Even a simple sentence like 'Today is Saturday' can be said a number of ways depending on the status of the listener. In English, there is only one word for 'You' which is used for everyone. In Japanese there is no word like this to refer to socially superior people. Titles like 'honourable one' must be used. Generally, family name (followed by *san*) is used, and the equivalents to 'You' are avoided.

Alcohol and greater informality

Only in certain situations can this behaviour change. For example, in some social situations, when drinking alcohol, people can forget the polite terms, and can complain and disagree. What is said and done must be forgotten when they are again sober. It is much more widely acceptable in Japanese culture to relax by getting very drunk than it is in Australia. Social drinking and entertainment are a part of a businessman's life. In a strictly hierarchical society, it is the only outlet for informality and frankness. If people drink alcohol, but remain formal and sober, they are regarded with suspicion. It is called 'Killing the saké' because it kills the pleasure of others.

Conversational response words

Japanese listeners give lots of feedback: they constantly exchange response words called *aizuchi* (which is difficult to translate directly into English, but refers to conversational response words exchanged frequently between

Japanese speakers). Many Japanese transfer this style to English and say 'Yes, yes,' frequently. It is important to know that this usually means 'I am listening carefully', rather than 'I agree', or 'I understand'. Japanese who are not used to English speakers will normally be worried if they are not getting any feedback, so it is a good idea to nod and say 'right' and 'mmm'.

Gift-giving, compliments and apologies are important

Gift-giving is extremely common, and is seen as a means of communicating the desire to build and maintain good relations. In many situations, it is polite not to open gifts at the time they are given (because this can seem to put more emphasis on the gift than on the giver). It is therefore wise to ask permission to open the gift immediately, and to explain the Australian custom (of opening gifts immediately) if in this situation.

Japanese are careful not to boast and not to accept compliments. When they deny that they have knowledge/expertise/competence, they may merely be being polite and modest. It is inappropriate to compliment senior people, because this suggests that the speaker is assuming the right to be in a position to judge the senior person.

Because of their preference for avoiding open unpleasantness, Japanese will seldom complain directly, or be openly critical of food or service. Instead, they will complain to the tour-guide, or to their friends, and not come back again.

In Japan it is good to apologise even when it is not one's fault. Apologies are made for causing inconvenience to others. It is not polite to make excuses. Often, instead of saying 'Thank you', Japanese apologise for putting the other person to so much trouble. Often gifts or complimentary services are given. This shows that the apology is more sincere than do mere words.

At the beginning of any second meeting, thanks (for help previously given) or apologies (for trouble previously caused) are expected. It is polite to follow this custom.

'In-group' communication may be more informal

Communication with 'in-groups' (family, friends and workmates) can be much more informal, and it is permissible to criticise members of the 'in-group', apart from people of higher status. Service people (such as shop attendants and taxi drivers) are regarded as of lower status because they are seen as performing a role for which they are being paid. This contrasts with Australia where they are viewed more as individuals, and treated as such.

Non-Verbal Communication

As with many other Asian cultures, non-verbal signals and unspoken assumptions figure prominently in the personal and business relationships of Japanese. The term *haragei* ('belly language') refers to the intuitive power to know what another person is thinking, by reading non-verbal cues.

Personal space is valued

Like other Asian cultures, Japanese culture is a 'non-touching culture'. In public, Japanese rarely touch each other intentionally. However, unintentional bumping is common in crowded public places, and people need not apologise for it.

Japanese prefer more personal space than is common amongst Australians, who usually stand about an arm's length from the person to whom they are speaking. Japanese prefer to be as far apart as the distance which making a deep bow would require.

Japanese are trained to avoid too much direct eye-contact, it being more respectful to lower the eyes.

Bowing and gestures

Their traditional form of greeting is bowing, although some Japanese have adopted the Western handshake when greeting foreigners. A person of a lower status must bow lower. Bowing accompanies or replaces almost all verbal greetings as well as being part of a response to offers, compliments and thanks. It is not advisable for foreigners to bow because it is a complicated ritual and is not easy to perform correctly.

As with other cultures, different gestures have different meanings for Japanese, and some gestures that are polite to Australians are rude to Japanese. It is best to avoid pointing and beckoning with one finger because Japanese use the whole hand for these gestures. For example, their gesture meaning 'Come here' is similar to the Australian wave of 'Goodbye'. However, Japanese do point at themselves: but at their nose, not their heart.

Some hints on polite behaviour

Because people want to maintain harmony and avoid any unpleasantness, they may smile (and even laugh) to hide negative feelings such as sadness, embarrassment and anger.

It is polite to pass things with two hands. For example, business cards (which represent that person's 'face') are given with two hands. They should be accepted respectfully, read carefully, and then placed somewhere secure. It is impolite to scribble notes on them.

In polite, conservative society juniors do not cross their legs in front of seniors, and women never sit cross-legged.

There are number of other behaviours that most Japanese see as very bad manners. They find them embarrassing, and even disgusting. Examples include the following:

▼ blowing one's nose in front of others (Japanese sniff), and using a handkerchief (rather than a tissue) for this purpose;
▼ showing the open mouth when yawning or laughing;
▼ public displays of affection (such as kissing in public);
▼ combing one's hair in public; and
▼ eating in the street (for example, ice creams).

To sum up

To sum up, when studying Japanese language and communication, it is important to remember that words and actions may not mean what they seem to mean, and that appearance can be more important than 'truth'. This is because tatemae behaviour is required, especially when dealing with visitors or superiors. This means using overt behaviour that hides what one is really feeling. The concept of tatemae is linked to that of 'face'. Japanese say that Chinese and French completely understand tatemae, but that Americans find it very difficult to comprehend, often seeing it as deceitful, and therefore reacting in ways that the Japanese do not expect.

It is also helpful to know that the normal, direct, 'get-to-the-point' communication of many English-speaking people is misinterpreted by Japanese, and other Asians, as being aggressive or rude.

Dining, Service and Accommodation Preferences

Dining Preferences

Dining out is popular

Japanese eat in restaurants, and drink in bars, a great deal. This is the way they meet friends, socialise with workmates, and entertain business contacts. They seldom invite people to their homes. This is because of the time taken to travel distances in big cities, and because their homes are usually very small.

Restaurants in Japan

There are basically three kinds of cuisine offered in restaurants in Japan: Japanese, Chinese and Western. Western food is well established, very popular, and available in great variety. This is especially true in Tokyo where the available food ranges from cheap sandwiches or hamburgers to very expensive French food.

Reservations are not generally necessary because there are so many eating places (usually open until late, seven days a week), and because people tend not to take a long time over meals. The 'bring-your-own' ('BYO') system is practically unknown in Japan. As a result, it is helpful to inform Japanese guests of the need for reservations in Australia, especially on Friday and Saturday nights. They should also be told about the limited opening hours of most eating establishments, and the term 'BYO' should be explained.

Japanese cuisine

Traditional Japanese cuisine is mainly restricted to rice, vegetables, fish and fruit. Food portions are generally small. They are beautifully presented and each flavour is kept separate. The Japanese call this style *sappari* ('neat, clean, honest and light').

Changing habits

A Western breakfast (consisting of black tea or coffee, and bread) is becoming as popular as a traditional Japanese breakfast. However, the traditional breakfast of *miso* (bean paste) soup and rice is still common.

These days, dinner is often a mixture of a Japanese dish (with fish as its main component) and a Western or Chinese dish (based on meat or vegetables).

Drinks

Beer is now the most popular alcoholic drink in Japan. Most of the beer drunk is made in Japan but imported brands are also common.

Whisky is also popular with Japanese, especially with businessmen. It is usually drunk 'straight' (that is, without being mixed with other drinks), or perhaps with only water and ice. Suntory is a popular Japanese brand. Bourbon is also becoming popular.

Saké, which is made from rice, is the best known traditional drink. It is usually served heated, but, in summer, it is sometimes served chilled.

Wine has started to become more popular in recent years. Women tend to drink more wine than do men. Women have started to drink more alcohol in the last twenty years or so, but they still drink far less than men.

Japanese sometimes like to try exotic drinks such as cocktails. However, they usually prefer them not to be cream-based or too sweet.

A good bartender catering for Japanese customers should make sure that soft drinks (such as orange juice) are available. Some tasty snacks or 'nibbles' (such as pretzels or rice crackers) should also be available because these are popular amongst Japanese as accompaniments to drinks.

Some hints for pleasing Japanese diners

From what has been noted above, it will be apparent that many Japanese are sophisticated diners who are willing to try new kinds of food, while, at the same time, having some general preferences and needs. To make Japanese guests feel welcome, the following hints may be helpful:

▼ Buffet-meals are popular because the Japanese guests can see what they are getting. In addition, they can be served immediately, and can have the size of serving they want. (Australian servings are often too large, with the average Japanese restaurant meal being half the size of an average Australian meal.)

▼ Japanese generally prefer meat which is undercooked by Australian standards.

▼ Short-grained rice is preferred. Rice and/or noodles should be included on menus, or made available.

▼ Unlike South-East Asians, Japanese do not mix rice with other food. It is used as a palate-cleanser between bites from other dishes.

▼ Freshness of ingredients, and attractive presentation, are important. Japanese do not regard Australian prices as expensive, but they do want top quality food. Australia has a reputation for producing an excellent range of fresh fruits and seafoods. Japanese visitors will probably wish to sample these.

▼ Desserts are not an important part of Japanese cuisine. Fresh fruit or ice cream should be offered as an alternative to other desserts.

▼ Japanese translation of menus makes ordering easier, but it is better not to have Japanese-only menus because this could be insulting to some.

▼ Japanese are accustomed to having soy sauce (Japanese not Chinese), toothpicks, iced water and hot hand-towels provided with meals. These would add to their enjoyment of meals here.

▼ Finger bowls should be provided whenever food needs to be eaten by hand.

Service Preferences

The customer is king

In Japan the customer is treated like a king. Japanese expect the same excellent service everywhere. They expect, at all times, polite, smiling attention from all service personnel. They also expect to be attended-to immediately when they approach staff for service. They think it impolite if staff speak to anyone else (especially another employee) while attending to their needs.

Japanese expect service personnel to take the initiative to offer help and to anticipate their needs.

Punctuality and speed of service is of great importance because Japanese visitors usually have limited time. It is wise to apologise for any delays, and to offer explanations, but not excuses.

Proper forms of behaviour are valued

Proper forms of behaviour are important. For example, correct forms of greeting are important in judging individuals and organisations. Japanese are used to being greeted by someone in a management position when arriving at a hotel. On leavetaking, the general custom in Japan is to see guests to the door.

Bowing is the most common way of showing politeness. If they bow, one should acknowledge this by lowering one's head in response. If a Japanese person offers his/her hand to shake, one should be careful to keep the handshake light, and judgments should not be made on the basis of the strength of the offered grip.

Appearance is very important to Japanese. Young children are taught to develop a sense of dignity, and to always look their best (because, wherever they go, they are representing their family). Japanese tend to be conservatively well dressed, and they expect service personnel to be similarly well dressed and well groomed.

Physical contact is best avoided, and it is therefore appropriate to put change in small trays and have keys ready in envelopes.

Some other hints on Japanese service preferences

▼   tipping is not a widespread practice in Japan, so many Japanese may not tip when overseas;

▼   care should be taken when seating groups: more important people, or older people, should be seated first, and should be allowed to choose their seats (because they usually sit in certain positions in relation to their subordinates);

▼ honeymooners should be asked whether they wish to sit alone or with a group;

▼ fast service is important; Japanese usually will not want to linger over their meal;

▼ in Japan it is the custom to lift the glass with both hands as someone refills it; waiters should be aware of this to avoid spillage and accidents.

Accommodation Preferences

Fast check-in and check-out essential

It is essential to have fast check-in and check-out procedures. Japanese guests often stay only one night in one place. It is best to have rooms allocated and ready, keys in envelopes, and porters to carry baggage to rooms immediately.

Many Japanese are not used to signing their names: they use seals. Some may not be able to write English. Where possible, arrange for tour-guides to be available to do the paperwork, if the guests desire this assistance.

Choices of rooms can be important

Groups like to be together on the same, or adjacent, floors, but prefer not to stay in rooms with numbers four (4) and thirteen (13) because of superstitions. For example, the sound of the *kanji* character for 'death' has the same sound as the character for 'four' (4). Japanese tend to avoid 'four' of anything.

Japanese who are travelling as a group like to have lists with room numbers and phone numbers for all members.

Japanese expect to be provided with plans of accommodation and service areas (such as restaurants). Lists and explanations of hotel facilities and local shopping (preferably in Japanese) should also be provided.

Attitudes to smoking may differ

Many Japanese men are heavy smokers, so 'No-smoking' signs should also be very clear and prominently displayed. They should incorporate signs, pictures or Japanese characters. Like many other Asian visitors, most Japanese find smoking quite acceptable, so they may be upset by some Australian rules and attitudes regarding smoking.

Cleanliness and hygiene are important

Clean, hygienic services and surroundings are important. The Shinto religion places a heavy emphasis on the cleansing ritual, and a clean environment is stressed in both public and private places.

Japanese prefer baths to showers, and bathe often. Communal (but gender-segregated) public bathing is an important part of Japanese life. It involves socialising and relaxing, but not washing of the body. Japanese find the habit of soaking, washing and rinsing bodies in the same water hard to understand, and may consider it to be dirty.

Approximately forty per cent of homes in Japan do not have flush-toilets, but have the squat-type set in the floor. This latter type is also the more common form of toilet in other Asian countries. Some Asian visitors might not like the idea of sitting on a toilet previously used by others, and may stand on the seat instead. Paper covers (showing sterilisation after previous guests) are advisable.

Some other points to note

Some other important points in making Japanese guests feel welcome include the following:

▼   twin beds are generally preferred to double or divan types of beds;
▼   Japanese are usually very concerned about security, and safes and door chains should therefore be installed;
▼   Japanese voltage is 100 volts;
▼   time is referred to by the 24-hour clock (as 1800 hours, 1900 hours etc.);
▼   clean, good-tasting water in the room is an important requirement;
▼   in Japan the ground floor is called the first floor;
▼   white flowers should be avoided in rooms (or on tables in restaurants) because they are associated with funerals in Japan.

Thais

Cultural Values

Thailand's independent history

Since its inception 800 years ago, Thailand has never been colonised. It is the only country in South-East Asia that has maintained its independence in this way, and Thais are proud of the fact. In dealing with visitors from Thailand, one should always be aware of the deep pride which Thais take in their independent history.

Thailand used to be called Siam until 1939. The name *Prathet Thai* (or 'Thailand') literally means 'the land of the free', underlining the Thais' intense pride in their independent history.

The Thai royal family

Since the overthrow of an autocratic monarchy in the early 1930s, Thailand has been a constitutional monarchy. The current royal family is very highly regarded in Thailand, and it is not acceptable to joke about them or criticise them.

Make-up of Thai society

The population of Thailand is approximately 59 million.

Of this population 82 per cent is Thai, although sometimes a distinction is made between the Thai people proper, who occupy the central regions of the country and make up 54 per cent of the total population, and the Lao people, who mostly live in the north-western and eastern regions of Thailand and make up approximately 28 per cent of the total population.

There are ethnic minorities in Thailand. Chinese make up the largest ethnic minority. Other minority groups include the Malay-speaking Muslims in the south, the hill tribes in the north, and Cambodian (Khmer) and Vietnamese refugees in the east.

In Thailand, unlike in other South-East Asian countries, the Chinese have not become the focus of ethnic rivalries. This is because there has been much intermarriage, and most Chinese have integrated into Thai society. They have usually taken Thai surnames, they usually speak Thai rather than Chinese dialects, and they are mostly Thai citizens. These Sino-Thais are present in all social classes, except those identified with military and government positions. They run much of the business and some are powerful behind the scenes because of their wealth.

Buddhism and Thai society

Most Thais are Buddhist (approximately 95 per cent of the population), and priests and monks are highly respected. The *Theravada* (otherwise known as *Hinayana*) school of Buddhism is practised in Thailand. This school holds the belief that only ordained monks and nuns can achieve *nirvana* ('enlightenment'). Monks are seen as the most important people in the country. They are highly respected and treated accordingly. It is taboo for a woman to touch a monk, or to hand things directly to a monk.

A basic belief of Buddhism is that the 'Path of the Middle Way' is best: extremes of happiness and sadness are to be avoided. As a result, Thais generally believe in being tolerant and easygoing because material things (and personal achievement) do not matter much in the overall scheme of life.

One's current situation is seen as transitory. People move through different transformations over several centuries in their quest for nirvana or the final state of peace. Because of this belief in reincarnation (or 'rebirth'), Thais tend to see economic status as the result of *karma* accumulated over the course of past existences, rather than as the direct result of current personal effort. They can believe that their current spiritual wellbeing is more important than their future career position. The Thai word *ngan* ('work') is evidence of this attitude, since it also translates as 'play'. Many Thais highly value *sanuk* ('the joy of living, a good time') at work, as well as outside the workplace.

As Buddhists, Thais believe that time is circular rather than linear, and there is no need to rush. People may 'drop-in' on one another at home or in the office. They can find it difficult to understand how English-speaking peoples think in terms of 'saving' or 'wasting' time, and in terms of moving logically and sequentially 'from Point A to Point Z'.

Chao Phraya River, Bangkok

The distinctive Thai culture

Thai culture, while distinctive, is an amalgam of Indian and Chinese patterns. Confucian and Hindu ideas, as well as Buddhism, have been influential in forming values and beliefs.

There can be differences in the values and behaviour between overseas-educated, urbanised Thais and their fellow countrymen. The former may have adopted a more Western lifestyle and some Western values. Generally, however, although Thailand is rapidly modernising, core cultural values have been retained.

Thailand is still predominantly an agricultural society and land is still the major source of wealth, power and social status. About 77 per cent of the total Thai population live in rural areas.

The family in Thai society

The extended family is the basic unit of society. Even where young people live separately, as is increasingly the case in the cities, old people are honoured and looked-to for advice.

One of the most important responsibilities placed on children is that of taking care of parents in their old age. This is a prominent feature of the Thai concept of family. Indeed, the primary concern of Thais is with their family. This is larger than the nuclear family (spouse and children) that most Australians see as their immediate family, but it does not include as many relatives and generations as more strongly group-oriented societies, and there is not such a binding sense of obligation to more distant relatives.

Family names did not exist until 1916 when they were established by royal decree.

An hierarchical society

Thailand is an hierarchical society with people ranked according to the status of their family and their age. This is accepted partly because it is believed that people have earned their higher status in their previous lives. However, in a service interaction, a customer has higher status than service personnel because they are buying this status.

Children are taught *krengja* which means 'respect' or 'consideration'. They should openly demonstrate obedience, humility and politeness. The younger, or inferior, person in any social relationship must feel krengja because it is part of the hierarchical system. In return, a superior has an obligation to put an inferior at ease.

The system does allow for some social mobility. However, there is a clearly defined role in each position on the social ladder.

In Thai organisations, the relationship of the superior to the subordinate tends to be autocratic and formal. However, under the surface, there is a close relationship because the superior is also supposed to protect and assist the subordinate in his/her private life as well as at work.

It is not uncommon for women to be chief executives of companies and there are many highly placed career-women. However, in general, women do not have social and economic equality, and traditionally they have been referred to as the 'hind legs of the elephant' (meaning that their proper place is at the back, behind men, supporting them).

The individual in Thai 'collectivist' society

Thais are more tolerant of individual idiosyncrasies than more 'collectivist' societies like Japan. They can better identify with notions of self-reliance and independence. In Thailand, there is not the strong sense of lineage, nor the veneration of ancestors, that is typical of cultures such as the Chinese and the Japanese.

Although there is an individualist quality to Thai behaviour, they do value personal relationships within their close groups, and aim for social harmony above all. They avoid direct criticism and open conflict. Children are not taught to be self-reliant or to defend themselves. They are taught to avoid aggression, and to stay out of trouble by running away. If a superior is hostile or unkind, krengja changes to *krengklua* (literally 'fear'). In situations where escape is impossible, self-control may break down and violence may result.

A 'rubber band' society

A writer (Fieg, 1989) has compared the rhythm of Thai life to a rubber band which is sometimes slack and sometimes very tight. This can be contrasted with American life which is more like a piece of string held fairly tight all the time. The 'rubber band' of Thai society is loose and relaxed much of the time. For example, Thais seem very easygoing and ready to socialise on the job. However, if someone with a higher status is involved, the 'rubber band' becomes fully stretched and social interaction is much tighter and more tense than anything comparable in America. In such interactions, Thais suddenly become serious and formal, and hurry to carry out orders.

Language and Communication

Verbal Communication

Languages of Thailand

Thai, Chinese and English are the main languages spoken in Thailand. English is taught in schools, and is quite widely spoken, but not many Thais speak really fluent English. However, if asked the direct question 'Do you understand?', they will almost always reply 'Yes'. This is done to avoid embarrassment for all concerned.

Status and language-style are linked

When one Thai meets another for the first time, each must quickly ascertain the other's status in order to use the appropriately deferential language. It is not possible to behave correctly until it is known who is superior and who is inferior. As a result, during initial small talk, questions like 'How old are you?' and 'How much do you earn?' are not considered impolite.

There are, in fact, eleven ways of saying 'You' in Thai, depending on the status of the person being addressed. Thais feel that having only the words 'I' and 'You' is too limiting. During the Second World War, the Thai premier suggested changing to this simplified system. However, the move was opposed and some people argued that it was an attack on their freedom of expression.

Avoiding negative feelings is important

Face-to-face criticism is seen as bad manners. It may also be seen as a deliberate attempt to offend. Public criticism, in particular, causes intense shame and loss of 'face'. If a superior criticises an inferior in public, this demonstrates the bad manners of the superior as much as it might show up the inefficiency of the subordinate person.

The expression of differences of opinion tends to be carefully avoided. People may take it personally if another person disagrees with them. When there is a problem, perhaps only 20 per cent of what might be stated is actually said. The rest is left to be guessed at, or presumed.

Being the bearer of bad news is usually avoided. In general, the most important aspect of social interactions is the psychological comfort of the people involved, rather than the objective truth of the matter under discussion.

'Hot heart' and 'cold heart'

Emotions should be hidden. Shows of dismay, displeasure, or even enthusiasm are frowned upon. It is considered especially crude, ignorant and immature to show anger. This is showing *jai rohn* ('hot heart') and one loses respect for this no matter what the situation. The ideal is *jai yen* ('cool heart'). This means not showing one's feelings and avoiding anything even potentially unpleasant. Speaking loudly is impolite, and Thais can see a raised voice as potentially dangerous. They may therefore concentrate on getting away, rather than listening.

Thai concepts of sincere polite speech

Thais rarely say 'Please' and 'Thank you'. 'Thank you' is kept for situations where one appreciates something very sincerely indeed, or when one is farewelling a superior. It is not used for small acts, or when people are merely doing their job.

There are many polite words in Thai, but they are different from English ones. This means that Thais might sometimes seem to be ordering or even demanding something, whereas, in their own mind, they are making a polite request. They might translate and say 'Pass the drink' but a literal translation would have been 'Help pass the drink a little'. Not all speakers would know it is polite in English to say 'Would you please pass the drink?'.

Cross-cultural misunderstandings can therefore be entirely unintentional, and an understanding of different language-styles can help avoid problems.

Thai greetings, names and titles

The common word of salutation is *sawadee*, which is similar to the Hawaiian *aloha*.

The very long Thai surnames (or family names) have been used for only the past fifty years or so. Given names come first and family names second. But only the first (given) name is used to talk to, or about, a person. It is generally preceded by the term *Khun* (which is the equivalent of 'Mr' 'Miss' or 'Mrs'), or, preferably, it is preceded by a title such as Managing Director. It is polite to refer to people only as 'Khun'. (The 'u' in 'Khun' is pronounced like the 'oo' in 'look'.)

Quite a few Thais in high positions have royal titles. These are usually written in abbreviated form. For example, P.O.C. stands for *Phra Ong Chao* (grandchild of King). Others include M.C. which is *Mom Chao* (child of P.O.C.), and M.R. which is *Mom Rajawong* (child of M.C.).

High civil servants have titles such as *Chao Phya, Phya, Pra* and *Luang*.

Non-Verbal Communication
Touching in Thailand

One must be careful about touching people, and one should never touch a person of the opposite sex. However, people of the same sex can walk arm in arm in public, and may touch one another in a freer fashion than Western men are used to doing.

The head and the foot in Thai custom

The head is sacred, being the place where the personal spirit resides, and it is therefore very important not to touch anyone (children and adults) above the shoulder. This social taboo is often unknowingly violated by Westerners.

It is considered discourteous to look over another person's head or to reach across the head.

People of inferior status should try to stand or sit lower than a person of higher status. For example, if a person of high rank were sitting on the floor, the only way to get past them would be to crawl. Thais say that this whole elaborate etiquette is not any stranger to a Thai than, for example, has been a man offering his seat to a woman in traditional Western society.

By contrast, the foot is the lowest part of the body, and it is therefore offensive to point with the foot, or to show the sole of the foot (which can happen by crossing the legs). When sitting, the soles of the feet should be placed squarely on the ground. A well-known Thai woman reformer and journalist was removed from parliament when she refused to uncross her legs.

Smiles in Thai communication

Smiles are highly valued, and the Thais are known as a smiling, friendly people. However, it is important to realise that smiles have more non-verbal meanings than they do in English-speaking cultures. Smiles can be used to say 'Excuse me' if something impolite has been done, to say 'Thank you' for small services, to avoid conflict before fleeing, and to cover embarrassment. Although Westerners will often combine smiles with appropriate words in such circumstances, this sort of 'smiling communication' may be entirely non-verbal amongst Thais. Thus, although Westerners usually give verbal clues as to the true meaning of their embarrassed smile (for example), Thais may merely smile, and give no extra verbal clue as to their true feelings.

Smiles are also used to hide sorrow. In the past, plays were put on at funerals, and other forms of enjoyment are still common on such occasions. An orchestra plays, and, after the religious rites, people play games (such as chess) and enjoy feasts to banish their sorrow. In this way Thais mix sanuk (joy of living) even with death.

The *Wai* as a Thai greeting

Thais normally greet Westerners with a handshake. However, the usual greeting between Thais is the *wai*. This involves placing the hands together at the chest and lowering the head. However, it is not as simple as it sounds, because it can be performed in dozens of different ways to fit the occasion, and to take account of the status of those involved. This greeting avoids touching, and reflects and maintains the hierarchical social structure. The wai is initiated only by the person with inferior status, and the superior may, or may not, return it, depending on the degree of social difference between the two. For example, people would never return the wai of a child, or the wai of a waiter who does this to express thanks for a tip. The lower the head and eyes, the greater the degree of respect being shown.

The right hand and the left hand

The right hand is used for passing because the left hand is used to wash with water after defaecating. An increasing number of people use toilet paper, but the feeling still persists that the left hand is unclean. Many Thais are left-handed, but they still avoid passing things with their left hand.

Eye-contact between Thais

There is not supposed to be direct eye-contact between persons, especially between persons of opposite sex. However, most Thais break this rule, so there is no need to avoid direct eye-contact.

Despite this more relaxed attitude amongst modern Thais, prolonged eye-contact should still be avoided because it can suggest anger or perhaps a sexual invitation.

To sum up

In general, Thais are concerned about the appropriateness of a wide range of conduct. Body movements should be controlled and respectful, and dress should be neat and subdued. One should always be aware of the importance to Thais of a range of non-verbal communication which would be unimportant to a Westerner.

Dining and Service Preferences

Dining Preferences
Eating utensils

Most Thais eat with a spoon and fork, with the spoon in the right hand carrying the food to the mouth. The fork is used to push food onto the spoon.

Chopsticks are rarely used except for eating noodles and spring rolls.

Thai cuisine

Chinese and Indian influences are reflected in Thai food, but there are also 'pure' Thai dishes with their own distinctive flavours. These come from ingredients such as *nam pla* (fish sauce), coriander leaf and coriander root.

Thai people often find Western food unappetising, especially large pieces of meat with no spices or sauces.

As in all of South-East Asia, the staple food is rice. The words for 'rice' and 'food' are the same, and everything else is called 'with the rice'. Thais prefer long-grained varieties of rice cooked without salt until dry and separate. A typical Thai meal consists of rice and a number of other dishes served together, often at room-temperature.

It is unusual to find salt on the table. Thais use the salty nam pla (fish sauce) instead.

Food is beautifully presented in the best Thai restaurants. The art of carving fruit into intricate designs (such as birds or flowers) is highly developed.

Politeness and eating habits

As in many other cultures, it is impolite to talk with the mouth full, to lick the fingers, or to appear greedy. It is also not usual to eat while standing or walking. Thais might be surprised to see Australians walking in the street eating food.

The evening meal is usually taken early (at about 6 o'clock).

Buddhist restrictions on taking life do not necessarily stop Thais eating meat, and even many monks eat meat.

Alcohol

Drinking alcohol is a normal part of social activity for men. At a business dinner, Thai men usually choose to drink whisky. Whisky is usually called 'Scotch' in Asia.

As a general rule, ice is not added to alcoholic drinks.

Some Thais may not drink alcohol because one of the five precepts of Buddhism is to refrain from drugs and drink which cloud the mind.

Service Preferences

Gestures and service staff

Waiters are beckoned with the hand, palm down, fingers straight and waving rapidly. Western service staff should be aware of this gesture when serving Thai guests.

Pointing is acceptable for objects and animals but not for people, so it is best to avoid this gesture when interacting with Thai guests.

Some other points to note

Some other points to note (when attending to the service preferences of Thai visitors) include the following:

▼   Cigarette smoking is common amongst both sexes.

▼   Thais divide the day up differently from the Western style. They have four sections of six hours each, not two sections of twelve hours. Nowadays they usually talk about morning hours in the Western way of counting time, but speak of evening hours in the Thai way. For example, they would say 1 o'clock in the evening when talking about 7 p.m. It is advisable to check by referring to the 24-hour clock with which Thais are familiar from timetables and the radio.

▼   Thais bathe often, at least twice a day. Showers are acceptable, but extra towels might be appreciated.

▼   Porters, bellboys and taxi drivers are all tipped in Thailand, and a good restaurant may add 10–15 per cent to the bill.

Americans

Cultural Values

The United States today

The United States of America (USA) is a federal democratic republic. It has a population of approximately 260 million.

The USA is an economic superpower, and many Americans have a high personal income and are keen travellers. Australia is one of the favourite destinations of American travellers, and the USA is one of the largest sources of visitors to Australia. From an American perspective, Australia is the number one preferred overseas destination in terms of individual countries, and is second only to Europe as a preferred regional destination.

A 'melting pot'

The American population is made up of many ethnic groups and there are large minority populations of Asians, Afro-Americans, Hispanics and Native Americans. Despite this, the USA has been a 'melting pot' and there is a dominant and recognisable mainstream culture. In many ways it is similar to other English-speaking Western cultures, especially Canada and Australia.

The importance of the individual

The United States of America is a society that places a much greater emphasis on the individual than on the group. Children are brought up to believe in self-reliance, independence, self-motivation and individual responsibility.

Americans generally believe in equality, but only in equality of opportunity (rather than in equality of outcome). Personal success or failure is seen as being the individual's responsibility, and a 'self-made' person (a person who has achieved success through their own efforts) is greatly admired.

Individual responsibility and blame

Americans tend to be extroverted (perhaps even somewhat aggressive) in their personal relations. This is generally exhibited in a positive way, although a greater percentage of the American population is in prison than is the case in any other country. Despite this, many Americans are practising Christians, and more than half the population attends church regularly.

Talking, arguing and fixing blame on individuals are important aspects of American culture. These features of society are, of course, not limited to America, but it is interesting to note that in the USA there are many times more lawyers (per head of population) than, for example, is the case in Japan. In Japan, harmony and working things out are more important values than are fixing blame or making individuals responsible for events (as tends to be the case in America).

Getting things done

In American society, there is a strong orientation towards activity, to 'doing' and to 'getting things done'. This is reflected in many common idiomatic expressions of American English. Common greetings are 'How are you doing?' or 'How are you coming along?' (in place of 'How are you?'). Americans 'take' a walk or a shower (rather than 'having' one). They 'do' lunch with someone else (rather than 'having' lunch).

In this same context of getting things done, punctuality and schedules are important. And the measurement of progress in getting things done is seen largely in material terms. Material possessions and material comfort is therefore highly valued.

Some differences between Americans and Australians

One major difference that can be identified between Americans and Australians is that Americans are generally more concerned about standards of efficiency, productivity and profitability than are Australians. Certainly, at least in the past, Australians have been more easygoing about standards. Their attitude has been 'She'll do' or 'She'll be right mate'. As a result, Australians sometimes see Americans as being over fussy 'nit-pickers', whereas Americans can see Australians as being sloppy and negligent.

The same applies to people performing a service. In the USA such people are treated more as a professional carrying out a service, rather than as an acquaintance on personal terms. Australians can see the way Americans behave towards service staff as being arrogant. And to an Australian, the service offered in the USA may seem impersonal and automatic rather than being what Australians would consider as 'genuinely friendly'. In a similar way, many Australian taxi cab passengers prefer to sit in front with the driver, whereas this would not be the usual custom in the USA.

A further difference is that the American emphasis on the Protestant ethic of hard work and individual virtue has meant less of a role for government welfare and charities, whereas in Australia there is a belief that the virtuous are not necessarily rewarded. As a consequence, Australians tend to believe that there is a need for mateship, a need to help one another and (in the view of some) a need to aim for equality of outcome as well as equality of opportunity.

In noting these generalised differences between Americans and Australians, it is interesting to note how Americans may see Australians. A handbook written for American readers (Axtell, 1991) presents a suggested list of characteristics of Australians. The handbook notes the following characteristics of Australians as seen through American eyes:

▼ called by some: 'Chicagoans with an accent';
▼ warm, friendly, and informal;
▼ firm handshakes prevail;
▼ speak frankly and directly; they dislike pretension;
▼ dislike class-structure and distinctions (for example, if alone, may sit in front with the taxi driver);
▼ value close personal friendships;
▼ use the word 'mate' often;
▼ know much about the United States, but feel we know little of them;
▼ will not shy away from disagreement;
▼ appreciate punctuality;
▼ have good sense of humor, even in tense situations.

Language and Communication

Informal and direct

In their verbal communication, Americans tend to be direct and informal, and tend to confront people directly if there is a problem.

This same breeziness, and often humour and 'kidding', can be extended to everyone. Americans are inclined to measure their social success in terms of how popular they are, and they therefore value general friendliness.

Despite this, first names are not used quite as widely as in Australia, and it is best to use 'Sir' or 'Madam' in service encounters.

American humour

American humour is seldom sardonic or negative. They can see Australian humour as too negative, and as being even harsh and offensive. They may be surprised when Australians laugh and joke in stressful, difficult situations and 'send-up' both themselves and their leaders. Americans are generally more respectful of their leaders.

Misunderstandings due to accents

American accents are much more varied than the Australian accent. Visitors from different parts of the USA will have quite different accents, whereas there are only slight regional differences in the Australian accent. Despite the differences in American accents, Australians are generally familiar with the different American accents as a result of exposure through American media.

The Australian accent has now become quite popular in the USA because of Australian movies, and many Americans are said to like to hear the greeting 'Gooday' pronounced 'G'die'. Some like to reply in the same way.

The influence of the media has thus greatly reduced misunderstandings between Americans and Australians due to problems with accents. However, despite this general familiarity with one another's accents, difficulties can still occur if people speak too quickly, or with little care for pronunciation.

One point about accents which is worthy of note is that many Canadian visitors dislike being mistaken for Americans, so it is wise not to assume that every person with a North American accent is from the United States.

Misunderstandings due to slang terms

Apart from difficulties with accents, communication problems can also be caused by slang terms. Although Americans are generally familiar with the Australian accent, they are not as familar with Australian (and British) slang terms. Service personnel should be careful to avoid using Australian slang words thoughtlessly because their American guests may not always understand the meaning.

In contrast, Australians are generally familiar with most American colloquial speech through the widespread influence of American television and films.

Misunderstandings due to idiomatic expressions

Apart from the problems which can arise with accents and slang, there are some words which simply have quite different meanings in American English and Australian/British English.

There are also words which Americans use, but Australians never use, or use rarely.

Many of these problems with idiomatic expressions relate to the hospitality industry, and service personnel need to be aware of these differences of idiom. Here are some examples:

▼ In Australia, the term *tomato sauce* means the same as *ketchup*; however, in the USA, the term 'tomato sauce' refers only to a special sauce for spaghetti.

▼ In Australia, the term *entrée* means a light dish eaten at the beginning of a meal; however, in the USA, this light first-course dish is called an *appetiser*, and Americans use the word *entrée* to refer to a main-course dish.

▼ In Australia, the term *serviette* refers to a folded cloth at the dining table; however Americans would always call this a *napkin*.

▼ In Australia, a *napkin* (or *nappy*) is worn by a baby, but Americans would call this a *diaper* (which is a word never used by Australians).

▼ Australians never use the term *drug store*, but Americans use this term to refer to what Australians would call a *pharmacy* or a *chemist*.

There are also some American expressions which Australians do generally understand, although Australians have other preferred terms for these things. Examples include:

▼ Americans ride in *elevators*, whereas Australians usually say *lifts*.

▼ Americans go on *vacations*, whereas Australians would usually refer to *holidays*.

▼ Americans travel on *journeys*, whereas Australians would talk of *trips*.

▼ Americans see *movies*, whereas Australians would usually refer to *films*.

▼ Americans buy things in *stores*, whereas Australians go to *shops*.

With all of these idiomatic expressions (and others not mentioned here), care needs to be taken by service personnel who should be alert to the importance of ensuring that they are communicating clearly with their American guests.

Dining and Service Preferences

Dining Preferences

Iced water

Americans are used to a waiter bringing iced water as soon as they sit down in a restaurant. Some see this as a means of getting acquainted ('breaking-the-ice'), and as a way to cleanse their palate before eating.

Food preferences

In many American-style restaurants, the servings appear huge by Australian standards, although in other kinds of restaurants they are similar in size.

Americans may like a salad before their main course.

The traditional American breakfast is ham and eggs, with sweet pastries. However, due to modern concerns regarding cholesterol in diet, this traditional breakfast is not as popular as used to be the case.

Thanksgiving

The very important American tradition of Thanksgiving Day is held on the fourth Thursday of November each year. This day of giving thanks to God is a national holiday on which schools and businesses close. People gather, usually in families, and enjoy a traditional meal. Roast turkey and pumpkin pie are among the symbols of this festival. American visitors who are away from home on Thanksgiving Day will appreciate Australian restaurants' being aware of (and catering for) this important cultural tradition.

Eating utensils

The American custom is to eat with the fork in the right hand. The knife is used only when necessary for cutting and spreading. The fork is then switched to the left hand. After cutting the food, they drop the knife, transfer the fork to the right hand and hold it like a pen to eat. Bread is often used to push food onto the fork.

Some foods such as French-fries and hamburgers are eaten with the hands.

Alcohol

When one orders a whisky in the USA, a bourbon will usually be served, so it may be necessary to clarify exactly what Americans want if they order a whisky.

Cocktails (mixed alcoholic drinks) are popular amongst Americans, and there are a number of famous and potent American cocktails. Martinis originated in the USA. Americans may enjoy a mixed drink before dinner.

American beers are generally less strong in alcohol than Australian beers.

Wines are popular. Ice cubes may be requested with white wine, but the common perception that Americans do not appreciate good wine is inaccurate.

Service Preferences
Detailed orders and queries

Americans tend to know exactly what they want, and American visitors can give very detailed orders. They expect these to be followed to the letter.

American visitors also tend to ask a lot of questions, and they expect staff to seek out the information for them if staff cannot immediately answer their questions.

High quality service

In general, Americans expect immediate, perfect and very attentive service. In restaurants of all types in the United States, staff always return at least once to enquire if everything is satisfactory. Americans' expectations of service-providers are generally much higher than those of Britons, Canadians or Australians. This is partly because of the American stress on high standards, but is also because service in the USA is based on tipping.

Tipping

Tipping is an accepted part of everyday life. Many service personnel depend upon it for a significant part of their income. This is one reason why service is so competitive and efficient. The basic rates are approximately as follows:

▼ waiter: 15% (20% for a group)
▼ bartender: 15%
▼ airport/hotel porter: $0.50 per bag ($1 minimum)
▼ doorman: $ 0.50
▼ hairdresser/barber: 15%
▼ taxi driver: 15%

A significant cultural difference

As noted previously, it is important that Australian service-staff understand that there have been difficulties in cross-cultural communication between American visitors and Australian staff.

In the past, Americans have complained about the service they have received in Australia, especially regarding the attitude of Australian staff, whom the Americans have seen as being disrespectful.

For their part, Australians have complained that they have felt demeaned by being treated like a servant. The staff have felt that the American visitors have been arrogant and bossy.

The differences are largely cultural. Australians expect polite requests, and expect to hear words like 'Please' and 'Thank you', even when being paid to perform a service. Americans say they do not understand the Australian attitude since the Americans are merely behaving as they do at home, and are treating staff as professionals who are expected to perform efficiently the services for which they are paid.

Similarly, American service personnel are more prepared to respect and work hard for a manager simply because the manager holds a senior position, whereas Australian service staff tend to work well only for managers whom they see as having acceptable personal qualities.

Improved cross-cultural understanding can alleviate these problems, and this difficult situation seems to be improving. According to a recent survey, the vast majority of American visitors were satisfied with the level of service and friendliness of Australians. According to the poll, while speed of service is considered important, efficiency and friendliness (as the Americans see it) are generally most highly valued. Continuing cross-cultural education, and satisfactory levels of service as a result, should continue to help this difficult problem.

Chinese

Origin of Chinese Visitors to Australia

In considering other cultural groups in this book, visitors have come from a single country of origin. In the case of Chinese visitors to Australia, the situation is not so simple. The overwhelming majority of Chinese people in the world live in mainland China, but Chinese visitors to Australia today come predominantly from other countries, states and territories of Asia (as well as a smaller number from mainland China itself). These other places include Singapore, Hong Kong and Taiwan. These various sources of Chinese visitors differ historically and politically.

Mainland China

Mainland China itself is known as the People's Republic of China. It is a huge nation with approximately 1.2 billion people (about 20 per cent of the world's total population). The main ethnic grouping, the Han Chinese, represent approximately 93 per cent of the population. Since 1949, mainland China has had a communist government, and this has limited its involvement with the life of the outside world. Nevertheless, it is a huge emerging tourist market.

Singapore

Singapore is a nation state in its own right. It was a British colony, and then (1963–65) was a part of the Malaysian federation. Since 1965 it has been a sovereign republic. Singapore has a population of approximately 2.8 million of whom 78 per cent are Chinese.

Hong Kong

Hong Kong is a former British colony which returned to the sovereignty of the People's Republic in 1997, although it has been promised special status as an economic territory. The population of 5.8 million is approximately 98 per cent Chinese.

Taiwan

The island of Taiwan's sovereignty is a matter of continuing dispute, with the People's Republic claiming it as a province, whereas the government of Taiwan refers to itself as the Republic of China. This dispute dates from 1949 when the Communists took over mainland China, and the former Nationalist government fled to Taiwan. The population of 20.3 million is virtually all Chinese.

Economic 'mini-dragons'

Singapore, Hong Kong and Taiwan are sometimes referred to as being three of the four Asian 'mini-dragons' (the fourth being South Korea). This term refers to the growing economic power of these states. The term 'dragon' is chosen because dragons are highly regarded in Chinese culture.

Apart from the three Chinese 'mini-dragons', many other Asian countries have substantial Chinese populations. Taken overall, about 55 million Chinese live outside mainland China. They control much of the wealth in the Asian region and, consequently, comprise a significant proportion of outbound travellers.

Chinese Cultural Values

With so many different places of origin, it is not surprising that Chinese cultural values today present an interesting mixture of the old and the new. We will first look at some of the factors causing change in older values, before considering some of the traditional features of Chinese culture which persist today.

Changing Chinese Culture

It is difficult to generalise about modern Chinese cultural values, particularly communication-style and notions of politeness. There are two main reasons for this. The first is the effect of different historical influences on the four societies discussed above, and the second is the effect of what might be called modernisation.

Historical influences on Chinese culture

Each of the predominantly Chinese societies listed above is different in a number of ways and has had different historical and political influences. Mainland China has been profoundly influenced by communism. British colonialism has had a great influence on Hong Kong and Singapore. The recent development of democracy in Taiwan has significantly affected that society.

All of these historical differences have had influences in producing modern Chinese culture.

Modern influences on Chinese culture

In addition to the different historical influences, Chinese cultural values are changing as many younger modern Chinese have attacked the old traditional ideas of indirectness, elaborate politeness and reserve, and have consequently adopted different styles. Indeed, it can be said that Chinese societies are going through a period of transition, and that new styles of communication and politeness may emerge.

Unchanging Chinese Culture

Despite the factors described above (which have tended to change traditional Chinese culture), it is still possible to talk about a traditional Chinese culture which persists today.

An ancient and proud civilisation

Chinese in all the societies which we have mentioned have much in common. The Chinese civilisation is one of the most ancient in the world and this has given many Chinese a sense of pride and self-confidence, extending even to a certain sense of superiority.

Something of this cultural superiority is reflected in the language. The name for China is *Jong Guo* which means the 'central country'. Non-Chinese were called barbarians, and a common term still used to refer to foreigners is *yang guidz* ('foreign devils').

Traditional values persist

Much that is innately 'Chinese' seems to have resisted the influences of history, politics and modernisation mentioned above.

It has been said by one writer (Bonavia, 1980) that Hong Kong is surpassed only by Taiwan as a community where traditional values have been

Nathan Street, Kowloon, Hong Kong

upheld and developed. And these values are still firmly implanted in mainland China, although they were violently attacked during the upheavals of the communist revolution with its ideology of equality and class struggle. In Singapore, the government consciously aims to maintain many of these values.

Confucianism, Taoism and Buddhism

The traditional Chinese value system is a complex amalgam of ideas that has evolved over the centuries from its roots in Confucianism, Taoism, Buddhism and other influences.

In some ways the main beliefs of Taoism are contrary to Confucianist tenets as Taoists believe that to seek knowledge and worldly success means 'to acquire', whereas to seek the Tao means 'to let go' and to try to achieve simplicity and emptiness. Taoism long ago adopted many of the features of Buddhism and Tao rituals imitate Buddhist ones.

One important idea of Taoism in Chinese thought is the concept of *yin-yang*: that all things are locked in a cyclical process and, as everything reaches its extreme stage, it transforms into its opposite. From this comes the belief in the need for a balance between opposites in all things, for example, between bland, cooling foods and spicy, warming foods.

In general, however, Taoism, Confucianism and Buddhism are complementary, and could be described as 'three-faiths-in-one'. Many Chinese accept Confucianism as a guide to daily living, employ Taoist practitioners for ritual purification, and use Buddhist priests for funerals.

Overall, Confucianism, which was the state religion or philosophy for 2,000 years, is the dominant ideology. Confucianism is not really a religion and most Chinese people focus on this world, not the next.

The importance of the collective

The core values of Chinese culture, derived mainly from Confucian thought, stress the importance of the collective: the extended family, the clan and the state. The Confucian values of harmony, strong interpersonal relationships and group loyalties, hard work, thrift and deference to age are all highly valued. A woman, for example, traditionally defers first to her father, then to her husband, and finally to her son.

The importance of education

Another important idea of Confucianism is that anyone can rise to the top of society through education. As a result, all Confucian societies still place great value on education. In the USA, the top universities have had to introduce quota systems to limit the number of immigrant students from these backgrounds. Confucian values allow an individual to work hard and strive for success but emphasise that the motivation is to advance the group, not the individual. Chinese can express their loyalty and love for their kin through hard work.

The individual and the family

A leading Singaporean Chinese politician has put it this way: 'The fundamental difference between Western concepts of society and East-Asian is that Eastern societies believe the individual exists in the context of his family. He is not pristine and separate. The government does not try to provide for a person what the family best provides.'

Relationships with 'in-groups'

In general, from early childhood, Chinese learn relationship habits that stress connection to others, the advantages of co-operation and humility, and the development of strong, enduring bonds with kin and other 'in-groups'. On the other hand, self-indulgent behaviour is discouraged.

The Old and the New: cityscape of Singapore with a dragon boat in foreground

Relationships are of great importance to Chinese. As well as the very strong bonds of the family (which include distant relatives), people often have close associations with old classmates, college alumni, and professional and trade groups. There is usually no need for written contracts when business is done between Chinese.

Guan xi

Guan xi is pervasive in Chinese societies. There is no equivalent term in English. It is glossed in dictionaries as 'to concern, to relate, to make connections, to make relationships'. Having guan xi (personal connections) is very important for getting things done (for example, getting children into a good school). Favours are rendered and received, and not returning favours is contrary to Confucian propriety.

It is said that the origin of many big business deals among overseas Chinese today can be traced back to shared birthplaces, dialects or past favours which have formed the basis for the connections and relationships which are so vital when doing business in Asia.

The extended family

The extended family has been the foundation of Chinese life and society for nearly 5,000 years. Ancestor-worship is common with many families having a shrine and photographs of their ancestors in their homes.

The elderly are revered for their experience and wisdom. In China, when a man or woman turns 60, they usually have a banquet, and family members make enormous sacrifices to be present. It is common for a successful businessman or bureaucrat to still pay formal respects to his parents (even if they are humble peasants), and to follow their wishes.

There are also strong ties to the ancestral village or home. When the communists appealed to Overseas-Chinese to invest in their home counties, they were appealing to strong tribal loyalties. Indeed, few invest in any other part of the country.

Language reflects importance of family

The language reflects the importance of the family.

There is a complicated and extensive system of kinship terms. For example, there are 16 possible terms for 'aunt' and 'uncle' which tell exactly where they fit into the family (whereas in English the terms 'aunt' and 'uncle' are vague about the exact relationship).

Another example of language reflecting the importance of family is that the family name traditionally comes first, followed by the given name for each generation. This makes it possible to place a distant relative in the family chain. The individual name comes last.

Current social life and the family

Traditionally the family has operated as a productive economic unit, maintaining solidarity and the shared goal of prosperity. In many ways, this continues today.

Private homes in China are usually spotless in contrast to the lack of cleanliness in public places (especially toilets). The emphasis on looking after the family's own interests probably explains this relative lack of interest in public places.

Filial piety (dutiful respect and care for parents) remains a strong cultural value. By tradition, children (especially the eldest son), have been trained to care for their parents as they become older. (Girls have usually left their family to join that of their husband.) There has always been intense pressure to produce sons to carry on the family name and worship the ancestors. In mainland China, because couples are permitted to have only one child, some female foetuses are aborted, or some female babies are killed at birth.

Although there are few arranged marriages these days, there is still pressure to marry and to choose someone from a suitable family background.

Modernisation is having an effect on gender roles, child-bearing, and child-rearing practices. The older view of women (as being important only for their role in continuing the male line) is changing. Women are become more independent and more equal within the family. This is particularly noticeable among Chinese living in the United States.

Language and Communication

Verbal Communication

The use of English

Many Chinese from Singapore and Hong Kong speak fluent English, as do the large number of Taiwanese who are educated abroad. In fact, almost all Chinese from Singapore and Hong Kong can speak and read some English, and many from Taiwan and China will have learnt at least a little (although they may not have had much opportunity to communicate in English).

All groups may have trouble with the Australian accent (at least in the beginning), and many will not know our slang and idioms.

It is important for Australian service personnel to be aware of these matters when speaking in English to Chinese visitors

Chinese dialects

While all Chinese read and write the same characters, there are different varieties of spoken Chinese, and many of these are mutually incomprehensible. However, increasingly, most Chinese can speak and understand Mandarin, the national language in China.

Cantonese, the dialect of Hong Kong, often sounds loud and excitable, even angry, to an English-speaking listener. Cantonese do not appear to value the pauses and low tones typical of the Asian style of communication. Nevertheless, it is generally true that speaking loudly is not polite in Chinese culture.

Li and the importance of 'face'

Traditionally, Chinese communication-style was governed by the Confucian concept of *Li* which dictionaries gloss as 'courtesy, politeness, respect'. It stresses harmony and forbids displays of uncontrolled emotion and lack of self-control.

Despite this, Chinese can appear quite rude and argumentative in certain contexts. For example, in the Taiwan Parliament, when harmonious control breaks down, extremes of anger and violent behaviour can be displayed.

This emphasis on harmony necessitates indirectness in communication, as do the concepts of losing 'face' and saving 'face'. Li and 'face' are closely linked, and people usually avoid doing or saying anything that would damage each other's prestige and self-respect. Direct criticism, for example, would do this, as would a direct refusal to a request. Obvious anger, sulking, or loss of self-control also cause loss of 'face'.

The personal feeling experienced in loss of 'face' is much stronger than embarrassment, and is better described as a strong feeling of humiliation.

Moreover, a broad range of things can cause loss of 'face'. These include: having an expected promotion fail to occur; one's daughter marrying a poor man; one's brother working in a lowly position; one's child failing an examination; and even receiving a gift that is not suitably expensive.

Smiling in Chinese culture

Smiling or laughing fulfil a number of purposes, including the covering-up of embarrassment.

The Chinese habit of laughing or smiling to cover negative emotions can be very disconcerting for Westerners. A Belgian woman who lived in China earlier this century observed: 'I cannot stand their laughter any more; they laugh when I cry'.

Indirect forms of expression

One feature of this desire to uphold the concept of Li is the tendency for English-speaking Chinese to provide extensive background material (for instance, their reasons for taking up a particular position) before coming to the main point. This can cause Westerners to 'switch-off', or to interrupt, and can lead to misguided evaluations of Chinese as illogical, evasive, or insufficiently assertive. In the view of Westerners, the Chinese are 'beating-around-the-bush'. However, from the Chinese point of view, they are feeling their way and attuning themselves to the possible reaction of their listeners.

There are no specific words for 'Yes' or 'No' in Chinese, and it is therefore difficult to be as direct as English speakers can be. One can only agree that something is right or not right. Chinese will therefore avoid saying 'No' directly to a request or invitation and, if they are forced to decline directly, they will lose 'face'. When Chinese visitors are dissatisfied, they will probably not be directly critical but they might hint at it in an indirect or generalised way. Culturally aware staff should be on the alert for this type of communication.

Language differences can cause problems

Despite this general tendency towards reserve, in certain circumstances some language differences can make Chinese appear inappropriately direct and rude to Westerners. This occurs because certain expressions such as 'How are you?', 'Goodbye', 'Thank you', 'Please', and 'I'm sorry' are used so frequently in English (even with friends and family) that they can sound overused (to Chinese listeners). Such frequently used expressions can suggest, to Chinese, a lack of sincere interest in people.

In contrast, some greetings and questions which are perfectly polite to Chinese can seem too personal and intrusive to Westerners. For example, common Chinese greetings include 'Where are you going?', 'What are you doing?', 'How old are you?' or 'How much did it cost?'. Although rather intrusive to Western ears, such expressions are acceptable questions to Chinese.

As a result of these language differences, Chinese might sound rude and demanding when speaking English because of:

▼ the lack of 'Please', 'Thank you', 'Sorry', 'Could you?', 'Would you?', and similar terms; and

▼ the tendency of Chinese to ask 'personal' questions which appear impolite to Westerners.

Singaporean English, for example, has features which are direct translations from Chinese, and therefore lacks many of the polite forms of Western English.

Names in Chinese

Forms of address amongst Chinese can be complicated. Certainly the use of given names is usually inappropriate. Among Chinese, elderly friends are commonly called *Lao* ('old'), followed by their surname. Younger friends are called *Xiao* ('smaller', 'younger'), followed by their surname.

By tradition, it has been a common practice for married women to keep their family name.

Chinese, especially in Hong Kong, often have an English given name as well. It would be quite possible for a woman to have a name like *Winnie Lee Chan Mei-ling*. Of these names, *Winnie* would be her adopted English name, *Lee* her husband's family name, *Chan* her family name, and *Mei-ling* her given name. It would be polite to call her '*Madam Lee*' or '*Miss Chan*'.

Care needed in translation

Care must be taken when translating promotional material into Chinese. For example, when Ansett Airlines began promoting its flights to Asia, the Chinese characters used to transliterate the name 'Ansett' could also be read as 'peaceful death'! The characters were subsequently modified to read 'peaceful speed'! And in Taiwan, the translation of the Pepsi slogan 'Come alive with the Pepsi generation' came out as 'Pepsi will bring your ancestors back from the dead'!

Individuals can differ

Despite all of the above, it is necessary to remember that individual Chinese, like individuals of other cultural groups, may adopt styles different from the traditional cultural values. Many individuals will vary their style depending on the social situation in which they are interacting. For example, in relaxed situations, and with intimates, many Chinese are voluble, direct and ready to argue.

Modern changes in Chinese communication

The traditional old style of communication is changing, at least to a degree. For example:

▼   it has been claimed that Hong Kong people smile only when they are happy;
▼   during the Chinese Cultural Revolution in the late 60s and early 70s, people were forced to criticise one another publicly;
▼   there are young Chinese everywhere who scorn the old styles;
▼   it is said that urban youths in China are noticeably more egotistical, assertive and self-absorbed than older people.

However, in recent years, the government in China has had to give encouragement to the strong desire for a return to social harmony, and Confucius is no longer vilified by the communists.

Non-Verbal Communication

Touching

Generally speaking, Chinese do not like to be touched by someone whom they do not know. A smile is preferred to a pat on the back or a kiss on the cheek. Some may prefer not to shake hands.

There is usually little public touching between sexes, including between married couples. However, it is quite normal for male acquaintances to hold hands, especially in China, as a show of friendship.

Pointing and beckoning

An open hand is usually used for pointing, and beckoning is done with the palm down and all fingers waving.

Eye-contact

Chinese, especially Overseas-Chinese, tend to maintain more eye-contact than many other Asians. However, winking at someone is impolite and can have bad connotations.

Anger

Chinese may show their negative response or anger by waving a hand in front of their face in a quick action similar to fanning themselves.

Business cards

Exchanging business cards is very important. It is polite to pass them with two hands, and to accept them in a similar fashion. It is also polite to read them carefully.

Personal hygiene

In China, spitting, and blowing the nose without using a handkerchief, do occur, although the government campaigns against these habits. People believe that they are ridding the body of a waste, and that these acts are therefore acts of personal hygiene.

Dining and Service Preferences

Dining Preferences

The importance of cuisine in Chinese culture

Food is central to Chinese culture. Chinese and French cuisine are widely regarded as being amongst the very best in the world.

Most provinces of China have their own distinctive style of cooking and much daily life revolves around food.

There is an old saying that 'while other people eat to live, the Chinese live to eat'. Indeed, it could be said that no people on earth (except perhaps the French) are as preoccupied with food as are the Chinese, for whom it has always been the first pleasure of life. The traditional all-purpose greeting '*Chi-guo fan le ma?*' ('Have you eaten?') is indicative of this preoccupation.

Food and status

Food is at the centre of, or accompanies, most social interaction, and the expense, status, value, quality and setting of the food often communicates more than does anything that is said. For example, the style of a dinner towards the end of a business negotiation can indicate success or failure, and can thus avoid a more direct message. Much that is hard or impolite to say is communicated through this channel, and no culture has developed the practice more than have the Chinese.

Food is a common subject of conversation. Confucius was a gourmet and wrote enthusiastically of the importance of food. A traditional gentleman was expected to be able to speak knowledgeably about food, its history and its preparation, and today many Chinese still see themselves as experts on food.

Dining habits

The food is the important thing. It is not usual to sit around the dining table after the last course is complete. People get up and go. A speedy end is good manners, although the bill should arrive only when it is asked for.

Like other tourists, most Chinese are prepared to sample typical Australian menus. However, it should be noted that:

▼   Chinese usually do not eat a lot of meat especially beef (many women will not touch beef), and they tend not to like big pieces of meat or undercooked meat. Lighter meals (for example, fish and different types of seafood) are more acceptable.

▼ As in Korea and Japan, medium- or short-grained varieties of rice are preferred, cooked without salt and served 'glossy', with each grain being well defined, but clinging together, so it can be easily eaten with chopsticks.

▼ Many Chinese do not like dairy products.

▼ Cold food is not highly regarded, and in Chinese cuisine only one first dish is cold. A cold main meal is usually not acceptable.

▼ It is advisable to have some Chinese food available, especially at breakfast (for example, Chinese porridge—*hsi-fan* or chuk or *congee*—or stir-fried noodles). Although it is true that many young Asians eat Western breakfasts (because such breakfasts are seen as modern, and quick to prepare), older tourists may welcome a more familiar breakfast.

▼ It is also advisable to have Chinese soy sauce, toothpicks, chopsticks and hot moist towels, as appropriate.

▼ Many Chinese are developing a taste for sweet things; Hong Kong has many tempting cake shops, and cappuccino and cakes are popular for morning and afternoon tea.

▼ Chinese generally see a close link between food and health. They may be particularly concerned about food when travelling because the actual travel is often seen as very tiring, not as an enjoyment in itself.

Australian Chinese restaurants

Australians should promote the fact that there are many excellent Chinese restaurants in Australia (especially those frequented by Asian-Australians) and that a good Chinese meal is cheaper in Sydney or Melbourne than in Hong Kong or Taipei (the capital city of Taiwan). The fact that many top Australian chefs are developing a new cuisine which is a mixture of Asian and European styles, using quality ingredients often available only in Australian, should also be promoted.

Drinks

Chinese often drink good brandy with their dinner, but they are drinking more wine and could be introduced to Australian wines. Sales of Australian wine in Hong Kong have increased from about 25,000 cases per year to about 100,000 cases per year in the ten years to 1996. In 1997 in Hong Kong, a bottle of cheap wine cost more than HK$100 (A$20).

Cognac, long the favourite liquor of choice in Hong Kong (and still so in Taiwan and mainland China), is being displaced because of health concerns, and because more women are becoming involved in business entertaining. In general, women tend not to drink alcohol. Offer plain hot water or weak Chinese tea instead.

Many Chinese will not touch iced drinks. They are seen as too cooling and therefore unhealthy.

The addition of Chinese tea to menus is appreciated by Chinese visitors. This green tea is a traditional accompaniment to Chinese food and different provinces produce different types. By tradition, alcohol was not part of the meal, and green tea is still the preferred drink of most Chinese at all times of the day.

Service Preferences

Good and bad luck

As with Japanese and Koreans, the number four (4) is an unlucky number, and this should be kept in mind with regard to service and accommodation.

Feng shui (the orientation of a building, and its ability to harbour good-luck spirits and deter bad-luck spirits) is an important consideration because people will refuse to live or work in a building for this reason. This is taken very seriously in Chinese communities, and personnel in the industry should be aware of this. It might be useful to get expert advice on feng shui when building or refurbishing accommodation which may be used by Chinese visitors.

Bathing

Some Chinese, particularly from the mainland, say they prefer showers because of their distrust of the cleanliness of public facilities.

Tipping

Tipping is a common practice in Hong Kong. Hotel staff and taxi drivers expect tips.

Until recently tipping was rare in mainland China.

In Singapore, the government frowns on tipping, although restaurants add a 10 per cent service charge.

In Taiwan, while tipping is not common, porters appreciate a tip for each bag carried, and taxi drivers expect to be given the small change.

Indonesians

Cultural Values

Ethnic diversity

There is great ethnic diversity in Indonesia. There are over 300 ethnic groups, hundreds of languages and regional dialects, and widely differing cultures within the one country.

In general, there are four broad ethnic groups:

▼ the majority group (who are of Malay origin);
▼ Eurasians, and people of Arab, Indian or Pakistani origin;
▼ indigenous peoples (not of Malay origin); and
▼ Chinese, originally brought to Indonesia by the Dutch colonists as labourers.

Indonesia is the fourth most-populous country in the world with a population of approximately 200 million inhabitants. The Javanese are the largest and dominant group. The island of Java has approximately 60 per cent of the total Indonesian population (about 115 million) in an area a little over the size of Victoria.

The indigenous populations not of Malay origin are very diverse and include such people as the Dayaks of Kalimantan (the island of Borneo) and the Irianese of West Irian (the western half of the island of New Guinea). Some of these people are, or were until recently, tribal.

There are approximately 3 million Chinese in Indonesia, and they play an important part in economic life. There have been tensions between Indonesian Chinese and other Indonesians.

Religious affiliation

Most Indonesians (87.2 per cent) are Muslims, but Indonesia is not an Islamic state.

Christians make up approximately 9.5 per cent of the population, Hindus about 2 per cent, and Buddhists 1 per cent.

There is an enormous range of Islamic observation, ranging from some strict, fundamentalist groups in western Java (Sundanese) and in northern Sumatra (Achenese), to the majority of Javanese who combine Islam comfortably with other earlier religions such as Hinduism.

The constitution of Indonesia guarantees freedom of religion, and belief in other religions is accepted by the Muslim majority. Religion plays a central role in the lives of Indonesians. To admit to being an atheist (that is, not believing in any god) is generally unacceptable in Indonesian society.

Hinduism is now largely confined to Bali.

The idea of *Pancasila*

The modern nation of Indonesia, which won its freedom from Dutch colonial rule soon after the end of the Second World War (1945), is made up of 17,508 islands.

The country's rulers have promoted the idea of *Pancasila* as a kind of State-sponsored philosophy to guide this widely scattered new nation. The five principles of Pancasila are:

▼ belief in the one and only God;
▼ just and civilised humanity;
▼ the unity of Indonesia;
▼ democracy guided by the inner wisdom of deliberations of representatives; and
▼ social justice for all the Indonesian people.

Pancasila is seen as important in developing a sense of unity and nationhood, as well as supporting the principle of freedom of religion in this predominantly Muslim country.

Difficult to generalise

In view of the many different ethnic groups, and the rapid modernisation taking place in the nation, it is particularly difficult to generalise about Indonesian culture. For example, some ethnic groups were more or less isolated from the rest of the world until this century. In contrast, the Javanese and Balinese have long had sophisticated, ancient cultures and much contact

Mosque, Java

with the outside world. The Balinese are predominantly Hindu. The Javanese absorbed Buddhist, Hindu and then, finally, Islamic beliefs. They have blended these beliefs together in their own, unique way.

Despite these differences, relations among the various groups are generally harmonious.

Indonesian culture is part of the South-East Asian cultural tradition which is distinct from the dominant northern cultures of the region such as India and China.

Gender roles

Gender roles and relationships are important aspects of Indonesia's distinctiveness from other South-East Asian regional cultures, and from the Islamic cultures of the Middle East.

Women are not protected or possessed as they are in more strictly patriarchical societies. By tradition, women in some areas such as Bali, West Sumatra, North Sumatra and Central Java were traders, and men shared in childcare.

Women can have powerful positions in government and business. This is further evidence of a more liberal attitude in Indonesia compared with many other predominantly Muslim states.

It has been usual for both men and women to make their own choice of partner and then ask for the permission of their family. Divorce can be initiated by either the husband or the wife, and there is no disgrace or limitation upon a future marriage.

A collectivist culture

In general, Indonesia is a collectivist culture which stresses deference and harmony. This is achieved by each person behaving correctly according to their status in society. While the individual must be honoured and respected, loyalty to family and friends is usually more highly valued than putting individual concerns or advancement first. It is the duty of the individual to obey the will of the group and the group leader.

Indonesian society is complex and interdependent. There tends to be a strong sense of obligatory membership of groups such as the extended family, neighbourhood groups and religious groups.

The importance of the family

There is a strong loyalty to the extended family. Members have an obligation to care for one another by providing emotional and financial support, and by spending a lot of time together.

Respect for elders is usual. Although most family systems are patriarchal, the Minangkabau of West Sumatra (despite being Muslim) have a matriarchical society in which the women of the family own the property.

The importance of harmony

Since Javanese comprise about 60 per cent of society, their values are important, and influence widely the social behaviour of other ethnic groups in Indonesia.

Javanese tend to mask their emotions. They will laugh and smile to hide negative feelings.

Harmony is regarded as the most essential value. There is a tradition of *musyawarah mufakat* (decision by consensus). The tradition of *gotong-royang* (mutual assistance) encourages a feeling of togetherness in both urban and rural communities. Individuals do not usually want to stand out prominently from the group.

The ideal for all sorts of things is that it be *halus* (refined, fine, polite). The opposite of halus is *kasar* (coarse, unmannered). A woman is behaving in a halus way when she talks softly and sits and walks in a quiet, smooth manner.

Business meetings and polite behaviour

As with other Asian societies, it is important to spend time on social courtesies and establishing relationships before getting down to business. In Australia, it is acceptable to telephone someone and say: 'Look, there are three things I need to discuss with you, and I have only ten minutes.' This would be impolite in Indonesia. Face-to-face discussions are preferred, especially in early dealings, with a considerable time being spent getting to know one another and deciding if a long-term relationship is possible.

This building of relationships is a very important factor for success in Indonesian business. One's position must be established at the initial meeting, and business cards are therefore essential. Patience is crucial and trying to accelerate the process tends to be counter-productive. When negotiating, it is best to aim for harmonious agreement, with any lobbying or disagreeing being done privately, before the formal meetings, perhaps through an intermediary.

Attitudes to time

Indonesians have traditionally had a relaxed attitude to time. *Jamkaret* ('rubber time') is a phrase which is used to excuse or explain lateness. However, being punctual or even early, is now being promoted nation-wide.

Language and Communication

Verbal Communication
Greetings

Formality of greeting is extremely important as a sign of respect and civility. The general custom is a handshake followed by a nod of the head when first introduced. After this, a nod or a slight bow is sufficient. The egalitarian salutation of *Selamat* ('blessings' or 'peace') is the most common greeting.

It is usual to ask questions about family, marital status and number of children. These help to place people. This is necessary before one can interact politely. For example, there are a number of words for 'You' depending on the rank or status of the person being addressed.

It is appropriate to ask visitors about which part of Indonesia they come from because they are proud of their ethnic origins.

Names and titles

Some Indonesians have only one name and no family name. Where family names are used, they can appear first or last depending on the ethnic group. Usually, however, the first name is the one that is used. For significant people, honorific titles are used, such as *Bapak* ('father') or *Ibu* ('mother').

Languages

More than 500 languages are spoken in Indonesia, but *Bahasa Indonesia* is the official and most widely spoken language. It is based on Malay, but contains elements of many other languages including Arabic, Indian languages (especially Sanskrit), Dutch, and English. There are many similarities between Bahasa Indonesia and the Malaysian language *Bahasa Malaysia* (*Bahasa Melayu*), but there are also differences in vocabulary and grammar. Service personnel should be aware that the languages are not identical, and offence may be given if the two languages are assumed to be the same.

English is taught as a second language, although few speak it outside the larger cities.

Indirect communication

Because the maintenance of harmony and the avoidance of any unpleasantness is so important, the style of communication generally tends to be indirect, even circuitous, to an English-speaking listener. Passive voice is used a lot. For example, people tend to say: 'A mistake has been made', rather than: 'You have made a mistake'. People often speak softly, and such quietness shows seriousness and respect.

Loud voices and shouting are especially offensive. Whereas Westerners tend to raise their voices, speak very slowly, and wave their arms about when trying to make themselves understood, all of these behaviours can convey anger to Indonesians. In fact, it is important never to show anger openly. The Javanese have a saying to the effect that only children, the mentally retarded and foreigners openly display anger.

A well-known Javanese proverb advises: 'Look north; hit south'. Civilised people do not say what is on their mind, but conceal their wishes and intentions, especially if in conflict. This is done in order to protect one's own peace of mind. The aim is to maintain a state of placid stability. In addition, it is not polite to make explicit requests.

In contrast to the Javanese, groups such as the Bataks are more direct. However, they may still be much less direct than Australians.

Smiling and stress

Indonesians have been trained to cope with stressful interpersonal situations by smiling in a non-assertive way. The angrier someone else becomes, the quieter and softer they become. When faced with conflict they generally keep calm, withdraw from the situation and deal with it later, possibly through an intermediary.

However, if a situation does become extremely stressful, and they cannot withdraw, they may react with violence. (To 'run amok' is an expression that has come from Malay into English to describe this behaviour.)

The word: 'Ya' or 'Yes' does not always mean agreement. It can merely indicate a desire to communicate and please. Indonesians often smile or nod in situations where English speakers explicitly say 'Thank you'.

Avoidance of bad news

Indeed it is important to avoid saying anything unpleasant. Bad or contrary news is not usually delivered directly. However, the Western tendency to explicitly identify problems (and possible solutions) is now more commonly accepted.

Individuals are not criticised publicly. This results in *malu* (loss of 'face'; shame). To make someone malu is to take his status away. Anyone (child or adult) who is acting as a representative of a family, school or business is told: *'jangan memalukan'* (that is, not to bring shame to oneself and others).

There are many ways to avoid saying 'No', one common way being to say *'belum'* ('not yet'). In English, Indonesians might use 'Yes, but' as a way of saying 'No'. It is best not to disagree publicly.

Silences

There is no pressure to make conversation, and sitting together silently is usually acceptable and comfortable. If there is silence on the part of an Indonesian, it is a mistake to believe that the silence needs to be covered up by talking.

Non-Verbal Communication

Smiling replaces words

Smiling is a very important and noticeable aspect of Indonesian culture. It is important to return the smile of an Indonesian guest. However, as with many Asian cultures, it should be remembered that a smile may hide anger, sadness, embarrassment or nervousness.

A smile can also replace the words 'Thank you'.

Eye-contact

Too much eye-contact should be avoided; in fact, prolonged eye-contact might be interpreted as a challenge. It may even provoke anger.

Significance of some parts of the body

Most Indonesians see the head as the place of the soul and, therefore, as sacred. The head and hair are seen as possessing *semangat* ('life force'). One never touches the head of another person.

The head is lowered to show deferential respect. By tradition, a person had to keep his/her own head lower than that of the person with the highest status in the room.

The left hand is not used to shake hands, touch others, point, eat, or give and receive objects. If it is absolutely necessary for service staff to use the left hand, they can make it less offensive by saying 'Excuse me'. To be particularly polite, things should be passed using the right hand, with the left hand touching the right elbow.

Posture

Standing with one's hands in pockets, or on the hips or waist, or standing with the arms crossed over the chest while talking, are all considered to be rude postures, especially in front of older people or a woman. It can be seen as arrogant and insulting. These are the traditional postures of defiance and anger in the popular *wayang* puppet theatre of Indonesia.

Crossing the legs is usually inappropriate, and the bottom of the foot or sole of the shoe should never face another person.

Physical contact

Indonesians value physical and emotional closeness to others. It is quite usual for men of all classes to walk arm-in-arm or holding hands. This reflects friendship and sociability. Women also follow these customs, but not to the same extent.

However, public affection or touching between people of different gender is most unusual. Such touching would bring shame to those involved.

Some other points to note

It is impolite to blow one's nose in front of other people, but sniffing is acceptable.

Pointing with the forefinger is seen as insulting. The right thumb is used for pointing. Beckoning with a crooked index finger is also rude. A gesture like a wave is used for this purpose. However, it can be impolite to call a person of high status in this way.

As in many other Asian cultures, opening a present immediately (in front of a giver) can be seen as 'greedy' and impolite.

Indonesians generally tend to be more formal than Australians and this is reflected in their dress. A degree of formality in dress, as well as in language and behaviour, is seen as a sign of respect.

Dining and Service Preferences

Dining Preferences

Indonesian table manners

Most Indonesians seldom use a knife. They usually eat with forks and spoons. It is better to offer them food which is already cut into small pieces so that using a knife is unnecessary.

Touching food, or passing it with the left hand, is not acceptable.

Indonesian cuisine

Many nationalities have lived in Indonesia over the centuries including Malays, Chinese, Indians, Arabs, Dutch and Portuguese. The ingredients and the preparation of Indonesian cuisine have been influenced by all these peoples. An attractive feature of Indonesian cooking is the habit of serving contrasting dishes. Each spicy dish is matched with one that cools the palate.

Rice is a staple food, and is always the basis of an Indonesian meal. The long-grained variety (cooked without salt, and served dry and separate) is preferred.

Most sweets are made from glutinous rice.

The type of food eaten varies from one region to another. For example, corn, cassava or sago are staple foods in some areas. In others a staple is sweet potatoes. Rice, however, is a basic dish everywhere and is the main course for most people. All other dishes are side-dishes. The word *nasi* means both 'rice' and 'meal'.

Some of the most common dishes are:

▼ *saté*: roasted chunks of meat or chicken served with peanut sauce or soya sauce;

▼ *nasi goreng*: rice fried with shrimp, meat and sauces;

▼ *bakmi goreng*: fried noodles; and

▼ *sambal*: hot sauce made from chilli peppers.

Of these, hot sambal is a common accompaniment with most meals. For Indonesian guests, it is advisable to have some hot sambal on the table, together with salt and pepper, because they might wish to add it to some Western dishes which they may find too bland or generally unpalatable.

Unlike some other Asian cultures, Western dishes which include dairy products are quite acceptable to Indonesians. Examples are thick cream soups (meat or vegetable), creamed vegetable casseroles and young vegetables pan-fried in butter. Pasta (with ground beef in tomato sauce) and potato salad (hot or cold) are also popular. These food preferences probably reflect the influence of the Dutch colonisers.

Fruit salad and fresh fruit are commonly served as desserts. However, other desserts such as chocolate cake, fruit cake, chocolate mousse/pudding and fruit pies are also usually well received. Many Indonesians, especially Javanese, like sweet foods in general.

In first-class hotels in Indonesia, both Western and Asian breakfasts are offered. A typical Indonesian range of breakfast offerings include nasi goreng, an omelette or salted eggs, a meat dish, bean curd, prawn crackers and fresh fruit.

Food restrictions

It is important to remember that Muslim Indonesians (and also some other Indonesians) do not eat pork or any pork products. They may feel uncomfortable even sitting at a table where pork is served. Orthodox Muslims do not eat pork, blood or the meat of any animal which has died through disease or other natural causes. All meat to be eaten should be *halal* meat; that is, meat which has been slaughtered according to Islamic law.

Balinese Hindus do not eat beef or any beef products.

The Sundanese of western Java eat raw vegetables (*lalap*). For others, salads and vegetable dips might not be acceptable. Most Indonesians find raw fish disgusting.

Drinks

Muslims do not drink alcohol and, in fact, many Indonesians are quite unused to drinking alcohol. Tea is the most common drink. Sweet soft drinks are also popular. Indonesian visitors will not usually want iced drinks. When tea or coffee is served, it is not drunk until the host says: 'Please drink'.

Service Preferences

Smoking

A very large percentage (perhaps a majority) of Indonesians smoke, and some Indonesian men believe that a failure to smoke shows a lack of masculinity.

As with other Asian visitors, Indonesians may find some Australian attitudes to smoking hard to comprehend. Staff need to be very tactful when enforcing 'No-smoking' policies.

Quick service

In Indonesian hotels and restaurants there is generally a large staff, and service is quick. Meals are not generally lingered-over in Indonesia.

Bathing and hygiene

Bathing is an important activity. Bathing at least twice a day is the norm, and talking about the pleasures of cleanliness is also common.

It is usual to bathe using cold water, splashing it over oneself, and wetting the surrounding bathroom area at the same time. These facts should be kept in mind when designing hotel bathrooms and providing towels.

Toilets are usually separate. In major Indonesian hotels there is a small hose on the toilet wall for washing after defaecating. In other public toilets, there is a bucket of water.

Tipping

Tipping is expected if there is no service charge. Taxi drivers and hotel staff expect small tips.

# South Koreans

Cultural Values

Recent history

Korea has managed to preserve its unique character and cultural identity despite being sandwiched between the vastly more powerful nations of Japan and China. Both these countries have overrun and ruled Korea at some stages of its history.

After World War II, Korea was partitioned into two countries, North Korea and South Korea. The Korean War (1950–3) was fought between North Korea (backed by the Chinese) and South Korea (backed by a United Nations' force composed of USA and Western allies' troops). After the war, North Korea continued as a strict communist society which, even today, has very little contact with the outside world. South Korea is a democratic republic. The war left South Korea in ruins, but rapid economic growth has lifted the standard of living to a level comparable to Japan and Taiwan.

South Korea (along with Singapore, Taiwan and Hong Kong) is often referred to as one of the four 'mini-dragons' of Asia. It is one of Australia's fastest growing tourist markets. However, only a small percentage of all South Koreans who travel overseas come to Australia at present. There is therefore great potential for further growth in this market.

Ethnically homogeneous

Except for a small Chinese minority, the people are all ethnic Korean, making Korea one of the most ethnically homogeneous countries in the world.

Like the Japanese, Koreans perceive nationality or citizenship as being equivalent to membership of the ethnic group, and have a strong sense of their difference from others.

Densely populated

South Korea is less than half the size of Victoria, but is one of the most densely populated countries in the world. The population is approximately 45 million.

About 57 per cent of the population live in urban areas, and Seoul is the fourth-largest city in the world with a population of about eleven million.

Rapid change

South Korea is changing extremely quickly. It is therefore difficult to generalise about modern Korean life. Exceptions and individuals who do not conform to such generalisations can always be found. However, whilst recognising the danger of generalisations, certain observations can be made about South Korean life.

Religion

There is freedom of religion in South Korea. In 1994, approximately 50 per cent of South Koreans followed a religion. These were approximately equally divided between Buddhists and Christians (predominantly Protestants), but the size of the Christian population is continuing to increase. Christianity was historically associated with the independence movement against the Japanese earlier this century, and, more recently, has been associated with the rapid modernisation of the country.

However, Confucian traditions (especially the key principle that social relations should be based not on individual satisfaction but on the harmony of the group) have most strongly influenced the behaviour of Koreans for centuries, and remain important today.

Hierarchical society

Korea is an hierarchical society with status determined primarily by age, sex, family and profession. Within the family, status is determined by the age of the male members.

Education valued

Education is highly valued and is seen as the path to success. Great respect is paid to well-educated people and to teachers at all levels.

There is fierce competition for university places, with the number of applicants being many times the number of positions available.

Family relationships

The family is the basis of society and is based on the male family-line. Family relationships are based on Confucian principles. Children are taught to be obedient, and discipline is usually strict.

Women leave their own family when they marry, although they keep their own family name. Ending a family line by failing to have sons is considered unfilial.

Although smaller 'nuclear' family living arrangements are now more common, the term *kah jok* ('family') still refers to grandparents, their sons, the sons' wives and the sons' children. The concerns of each member of this group are the concern of all.

The oldest male generally has the final say in important matters. Since South Korea does not have any nationwide insurance for the aged, the first son and his wife are responsible for caring for the parents when they retire. He should also pay for the education and marriages of his younger siblings if his father cannot do so.

The joining of two people in marriage (and therefore the joining of two families) is probably the most important occasion in a Korean's life, apart from the first and sixtieth birthdays. A sizeable minority of marriages are still arranged by a matchmaker although 'love-marriages' are now preferred by the young.

Gender roles

According to Confucian tradition, women have to obey three men: father, husband and son.

Recently South Korean women have begun to demand a more active role outside the home, assistance with work in the home, and a more 'romantic' relationship, but men tend not to be eager to accept such changes. Nevertheless, increasing numbers of women now participate in the workforce, and it is against the law to discriminate against them. Few women have yet reached the top echelons in business, and many men still do not willingly report to a female supervisor.

Although traditional Korean society has insisted upon female submission to men, women usually manage the family finances, and are responsible for the wellbeing of the family.

Attitudes to time

While it is no longer acceptable to be late for appointments, building up good relations and trust is more important than getting business done in a hurry.

Language and Communication

Verbal Communication

The Korean language

The Korean language has its own phonetic alphabet, *hangul*. This script is often mixed with Chinese characters in newspapers and government documents. The Korean language is similar to Japanese in that sentences end with the verb.

Although numerous words from Chinese have been adapted into Korean, and although Chinese characters are still used, there is no similarity in grammar.

English in South Korea

English is taught in schools, but the real level of comprehension of many English-speaking South Koreans may not be as good as their polite responses might suggest.

Korean family names and titles

As in Chinese, there are numerous terms which exactly define the position of people in the family. Also, as in Chinese, the family name comes before given names. The family name is usually a one-syllable name, and is followed by a one- or two-syllable given name, with the first syllable often being the clan or generation name.

There are some very common family names (for example, *Kim*, *Lee* or *Yi*, *Park* or *Pak*, *Ch'oe* and *Chong*). One in four Koreans is named *Kim*, and more than half are named *Kim, Lee* or *Park*. In the past this has caused problems for some young couples who fell in love with someone with the same surname and the same ancestors. According to an ancient Confucian law, everybody sharing the same clan name and regional ancestry (even many generations ago), is still considered family, and therefore cannot marry. Nowadays, however, many exceptions are made to this rule.

Titles such as 'President' and 'Managing Director' are used whenever known. Some Koreans may put their family name last when introducing themselves to Westerners. It is impolite to use given names, except for very young children (or between close friends).

Harmony and respect is valued

Interpersonal relationships operate on the principle of harmony, and this, in turn, affects communication. It is more important to maintain a peaceful, pleasant atmosphere than to tell the complete truth or to attempt to achieve your immediate goals.

The concept of *kibun* is central here. Although there is no exact equivalent word in English, the term refers to a person's mood or current state of mind. To hurt someone's kibun causes loss of 'face' to the extent of personal humiliation. Kibun enters into every aspect of life. Knowing and preserving the state of another's kibun (along with one's own) is most important. A person's kibun can be hurt in many ways, as, for example, if a subordinate does not show enough respect, or hands something with the left hand. The higher a person's status, the greater this sensitivity, and the greater the humiliation suffered.

Sensitivity to others

Another important concept is *nunchi* (which is the ability to sense another's kibun). Because Koreans have been trained to control their emotions, and to disguise their true feelings (for example, to laugh when uncomfortable and to smile when nervous or sad), this nunchi is a special skill. As with other Asian cultures this behaviour is related to the strong desire to gain and save 'face'. Formality and conformity prevent embarrassing situations, and conflicts are resolved privately, preferably without loss of 'face' for anyone. It used to be said that Koreans feared loss of 'face' (*ch'aemyon*) more than they feared the death of a spouse, although nowadays people tend to see this as an exaggeration.

Emotionalism of Koreans

Despite what has been noted above, it is said that what most distinguishes Koreans from Japanese or Chinese is the relative emotionalism of the Koreans. While they may not always display this emotionalism, it is said to strongly influence their behaviour, even their business decisions.

Avoidance of conflict

An important aspect of communication which stems from Confucianism is a humble attitude, which Koreans like to maintain, and which they admire in others. Open criticism and public disagreement are considered very serious, and such attitudes should be expressed only in an indirect way. Bad news and adverse opinions are often repressed, or revealed only with great care at the most propitious time.

When anger is openly expressed, it can be quite strong, and any expression of anger or criticism certainly indicates much greater dissatisfaction than any equivalent behaviour on the part of a Westerner.

Getting to know strangers

In getting to know one another, questions about such matters as marital status and number of children are not seen as being too personal, but are acceptable.

In Western societies such as Australia, there tend to be rules for relating to strangers, such as orderly queuing, and 'first-come, first-served'. In certain situations Westerners might smile and greet strangers, introduce themselves, offer help, or start up a friendly conversation. Such behaviour is unusual in Korea. For example, introductions are generally made by an intermediary, and then only for a specific purpose.

Once people are introduced a relationship is established. People have to put a great deal of time, money and energy into relationships, whereas strangers tend to be viewed as less important, and can be treated quite differently. For example, an apology is not usually made if strangers are unintentionally bumped or stepped-upon.

Silences in conversation

Koreans appear to be more comfortable with silence than is the case with most Westerners. Two friends might enjoy one another's company without speaking for long periods. People sense emotions. Putting the feeling into words is thought to make the emotion more trivial.

It is quite acceptable to enjoy a meal in silence, and then perhaps socialise afterwards. Pauses between taking turns in a conversation are common, and it is therefore important to wait for these pauses when talking with a Korean.

Vigorous action and animation can be seen as lack of manners.

Non-Verbal Communication

Composure maintained

As with all peoples, Koreans laugh and smile when they are happy or amused. But, like some other cultural groups, it is also quite common for them to maintain composure when they feel sorrow, embarrassment, anger or shame.

Negative gesture

Koreans, like many other Asians, avoid saying 'No', but they may tip their head back and audibly suck air in through their teeth to signal 'No', or that something is very difficult.

Eye-contact

Eye-contact is made much less frequently than is the case between Westerners in conversation, and it is polite to look down in certain situations such as when a superior is displeased.

Normally Koreans look to either side when not keeping eye-contact. When one or both are angry, or during a business transaction, long eye-contact is more common.

Touching

Whereas touching older people or members of the opposite sex is generally not appropriate, it is not unusual to see members of the same sex (especially young people) holding hands or touching one another in affectionate ways. This indicates nothing more than friendship.

Passing and receiving objects

When passing and receiving something (particularly to seniors) it is polite to use both hands. Alternatively, the right hand can be used alone, but grasped at the wrist or forearm by the left.

Greeting

The manner of greeting depends on age and status. A bow is the traditional greeting, but men usually also shake hands. They may support their right arm with their left hand to show respect.

Business cards are important, and are presented and accepted with both hands.

Some other points to note

Apart from the points noted above, some other important aspects of Korean non-verbal communication include the following:

▼ By tradition, women have covered their mouth when smiling, and people still tend to cover their mouth when yawning or using a toothpick.

▼ As with other Asian cultures, pointing and beckoning (with the hand) is best avoided with Koreans. Their beckoning gesture is waving the fingers of the hand (with the palm down).

▼ Because it is awkward for Koreans to talk to strangers they tend to use non-verbal communication. For example, if a person standing on a bus is carrying a heavy load, it is polite for a person who is seated to offer to hold it. This offer is made, not by speaking, but by tugging at the load.

Dining and Service Preferences

Dining Preferences

Korean cuisine

Koreans will try different kinds of food, especially if it is fresh and light. Tropical fruit and fish are popular.

Korean food is generally spicy. It is quite different from Chinese and Japanese food. There is no distinction made between breakfast, lunch and dinner food. By tradition, all the food is put on the table at the same time. Rice is always served, and a meal is not considered a meal if there is no rice. However, at breakfast, rice is sometimes served as a porridge. Short-grained rice (the partially sticky type which Japanese also eat) is preferred.

The rice is almost always accompanied by *kimch'i* which is a spicy pickled dish of which the chief ingredients are Korean cabbage and radish. These are stuffed or mixed with spices such as red peppers, fresh ginger, garlic, shallots and often pickled shellfish or fish. There are more than 100 different types of kimch'i. Many Koreans eat this type of food every day. Other foods are pickled in the same way. Hot soup is also commonly served.

Beef is the most popular meat. It is usually thinly sliced and marinated. Pork and chicken are also common, but mutton is seldom eaten.

The seven basic flavours of Korean food are garlic, ginger, black pepper, spring onions, soy sauce, sesame oil and roasted sesame seeds. It is advisable to have some similar sauces on the table in addition to salt and pepper.

Meals do not typically end with sweets, although fresh fruit (cut into small pieces and eaten with a fork or toothpick) is often served. Cakes such as steamed rice cakes, or a deep-fried cookie (made of flour, sesame oil and honey), may be served on special occasions. Cheese is eaten by some children, but usually not by adults.

Eating utensils

A spoon and chopsticks are used for eating. Eating any food with the fingers is seen as impolite. Everything is eaten from bowls, not plates.

Table manners

Nose-blowing and sneezing are unacceptable, particularly at the table, but sniffing is acceptable.

Social expenditure counts in terms of status, and a lot of entertaining is done in restaurants and nightclubs. As in many other collectivist cultures, offering to pay a share of the cost is not done. The person who has extended the invitation to the function would be offended.

Tea

Koreans (like Chinese) are keen tea-drinkers. Besides the green tea made from Chinese tea leaves, there are many Korean teas. Ginseng tea made from the thinly sliced ginseng root, and, mixed with honey, is processed into powder and exported worldwide. Other teas served in Korean tea houses include teas made from ginger, arrowroot plant and a variety of fruits. It is advisable to offer at least one variety of Korean tea to guests.

Alcohol

Although younger South Koreans are drinking less alcohol now, drinking alcohol is important for males for social and business reasons, and South Korea has one of the highest per capita rates of alcohol consumption in the world.

It is often felt that one really gets to know a person only when they are 'under the influence' and, as a result, lower their defences. As with the Japanese (but not with other Asian cultures) becoming very drunk is acceptable, and much bad behaviour is excused when people are drunk. Indeed, it has been claimed that a major South Korean company has been known to hold a 'Mind-Opening Day' when staff members can drink a lot of whisky and express their opinion to anyone in the company (colleagues or superiors). Next day it is back to the status quo.

Women, generally, do not drink alcohol, and those who do are usually moderate drinkers. If they wish, older women are free to smoke, and to drink alcohol, as they never could when young.

There are rules of etiquette in drinking. For example, one should not pour drink into a partly filled glass, nor pour one's own drink. Drinks are poured with the right hand supported by the left, and glasses are received with both hands. Glasses are sometimes exchanged, this being symbolic of the family spirit that Koreans value.

Whisky is popular, as are beer and wine.

Appetisers such as dried beef, dried fish, nuts or fruit are always served with drinks.

Water is served at the end of the meal.

Singing while drinking is an old custom and karaoke bars are popular.

Service Preferences

Unlucky number

As with the Japanese and Chinese, four (4) is an unlucky number, so it is best to avoid putting Koreans on the fourth floor.

Tipping

Koreans generally appreciate friendly, efficient service. Tipping is not widespread in South Korea. Usually a 10 per cent service charge, and a 10 per cent tax, are added to hotel and restaurant bills.

Germans

Cultural Values

Population and ethnic make-up

Germany has a total population of about 81 million. After the Second World War, Germany was partitioned into East and West. The East was ruled by a strict communist government until it collapsed in 1989. Despite the problems of integrating East and West Germany since reunification in 1990, Germany is still one of the world's most affluent societies

The population is overwhelmingly made up of ethnic Germans whose numbers are not increasing. However, immigrant populations (including refugees from all over the world) are growing.

German tourists to Australia

Germans rank second on the list of the world's top tourism spenders. They enjoy relatively high salaries and long holidays (6–8 weeks per year).

The number of German tourists to Australia has been increasing every year.

German tourists enjoy remote areas and see more of Australia than any other nationality.

Religion

About 45 per cent of Germans are Protestant Christians, the great majority of whom are Lutherans. Most of the Protestants live in the north. About 40 per cent of the people are Roman Catholics, concentrated in the Rhineland and Bavaria. About 2 per cent are Muslim. Approximately 30,000 Jews live in Germany today.

More than 96 per cent of Germans say that they belong to a religion. However, in general, Germans are not regular churchgoers.

The individual and society

Although Germans believe in individuality, there is more emphasis on collectivism and conformity than is the case in Australia, although less so than in most Asian societies. Each individual is expected to contribute to society to the best of their ability. Germans believe in the importance of rules and order in society, and public signs proclaiming acceptable behaviour are common.

German society can be likened to a symphonic orchestra. An orchestra, like society, is made up of individuals with their own likes and dislikes. However, for the greater good (that is, the music), individual preferences are subdued to the overall needs of the symphony. Symphonic music was created as an art form in Germany in the 16th century, and the precision and synchronicity that characterise it make a suitable metaphor for modern Germany.

Industrious and ordered society

Germans have a reputation for being industrious and thrifty. Order, responsibility and achievement are highly valued. People are generally very law-abiding. Those who disregard the rules may be criticised by total strangers in public. For instance, if someone walks against a red light when there is no traffic, others may show disapproval quite openly.

Education

German people are generally well educated and well informed. Their education system has a reputation for excellence, and the level of literacy in Germany is very high. The education system is based on the imparting and acquiring of huge amounts of knowledge, as well as teaching students to develop their own opinion.

People appreciate intelligent conversation and discussions can become very lively. It is not considered rude to express a different opinion, although the expression of different opinions is less common than is the case in Australia.

Formality and punctuality

Formality in both behaviour and appearance has traditionally been highly valued. However, many people today prefer a more informal style, and some Germans claim that in certain workplaces there is more informality than is the case in Australia.

In general, punctuality is very important, and guests are expected to be on time.

Privacy

There is a strong emphasis on privacy in German society.

By tradition, houses in some areas were built with the front door made up of two parts, with only the top half being opened to receive goods, or to converse with neighbours. Even today, houses tend to be hidden by fences and hedges.

There is a great love of the outdoors, and gardens or yards are a central part of an ideal home. However, they are usually at the back, well hidden from the neighbours by trees and shrubbery.

People seldom 'drop-in' on one another, and time periods for making a noise may be prescribed. Police could be called if people made a lot of noise late at night. Many Germans are very careful to phone only at certain times, in order to disturb others as little as possible.

Order and cleanliness

Cleanliness and order are important; a rental lease may well require a tenant to sweep and clean the footpath, and any other nearby public areas.

Language and Communication

Verbal Communication

Language

German is spoken by everyone.

Standard German is taught in the schools, and used in the media. However, in different regions, various dialects may be spoken. Indeed people speaking different dialects may have difficulty understanding each other.

English is widely understood. Every child learns English from the age of nine.

Forms of address and greeting

German formality and social distance are reflected in their forms of address. First names are used only with people with whom one is intimate. Housewife-neighbours talking together refer to each other (and to others about whom they are speaking), as *Frau* (Mrs) plus surname. The title *Fraulein* (Miss) is no longer used for unmarried women.

Titles are widely used to identify a person's position in the social structure. For example, a physician and professor (whose surname was Kaempfer) would be addressed as *Herr Professor Doktor* Kaempfer.

The most common form of greeting is *Guten Tag* ('Good Day'). *Hallo* ('Hello') is also common between friends. It has been observed that Germans view 'the weather' as a stupid topic of conversation, and do not reciprocate when asked 'How are you?'.

Problems with translation difficulties

Requests in German may sound rude if directly translated into English because Germans do not use forms such as 'Could you … ?' and 'Would you mind … ?'. Rather, a direct translation comes out as 'You will bring me a glass of water!'. It is therefore understandable that Germans can be judged to be rude and arrogant when in fact they are merely using the English forms that are equivalent to those they would use in their own language. They have no intention of being rude.

The opposite can also cause problems. Research has been done at Macquarie University looking at what happens when German people live in Australia for a long time and then return to Germany. They may have trouble communicating with their family and old friends. For example, a German woman who had lived in Australia for fifteen years returned home to visit her mother. Her mother became terribly upset and said that her daughter no longer loved her. The problem was the daughter's use of Australian-style expressions like: 'Would you like a cup of tea?' or 'Would you mind if I opened the window?'. Such sentences sound ridiculously formal in German.

It is also important to be careful about using humour. Often it does not translate well and Germans may think that the speaker is being too familiar or rude.

Non-Verbal Communication
Greetings

A fairly firm but brief handshake is the norm among men and women. Children also often offer their hand in greeting. Kissing on the cheek is rare, and is usually reserved for close friends or relatives.

Formality is preferred

Because many Germans tend to prefer more proper behaviour, Australian informal behaviour can be seen as inappropriate, or even as being rude behaviour by German visitors.

Examples include:

▼ talking with hands in pockets;
▼ putting legs or feet up on furniture; and
▼ pointing with the index finger to one's own head (an especially inappropriate gesture as this is seen as insulting to another person).

Dining and Service Preferences

Dining Preferences

Table manners

The continental style of eating is used. The fork is held in the left hand, and the knife in the right, as in Australia. People very seldom eat with their fingers.

Hands are kept above the table with wrists resting on the table edge. It is not 'proper' behaviour to have one's hands under the table.

Cuisine

As with many societies, dietary preferences vary from region to region. Nevertheless, potatoes, noodles, dumplings, sauces, vegetables, cakes and pastries are generally very popular foods, as are a variety of sausages, pork, chicken and other meats. Meat consumption is much lower than in Australia, and vegetarian dishes are increasingly popular, especially amongst young people and women. However, most older people still probably prefer a meal comprising a good-sized piece of meat accompanied by potatoes and other cooked vegetables. The traditional sausage is not as popular these days, since they contain much fat.

It should be remembered that many Germans are cosmopolitan and want to try new types of food. Although men, especially, love their beer, and fried sausages can be bought everywhere (as chips are in Australia), Germans might take exception to the stereotype that they always want to drink beer and eat sausages. Would all Australians like to be thought of as wanting to swill only beer and eat only meat pies?

Dining outdoors

In Germany, meals and snacks are eaten outdoors at all times of the day. The *Biergarten* ('beer garden') and other garden restaurants are popular venues for entertaining guests and meeting friends and families.

Drinks

Most Germans prefer beer, wine or mineral water with meals.

Soft drinks and fruit juices are also popular.

People seldom drink tap water (although the water in Germany is exceptionally clean), and they generally prefer drinks without ice.

Service Preferences

Efficiency valued

Germans usually expect fast, efficient 'no-nonsense' service. They do not expect to be kept waiting and a very good excuse is needed to pacify them in such a situation.

One German student described it this way: 'We are not as patient as Australians. If you want to have an upset customer then let a German wait. We get red in the face and turn our back and, for sure, we don't come back.'

However, once the meal has been served, Germans enjoy eating their meals slowly.

Neatness and tidiness

A neat and tidy appearance is essential in terms of both staff and surroundings. Any untidiness or disorganisation is seen as incompetence.

Cleanliness is highly valued. For example, a dirty mark on a glass, or bed linen that is not spotless, will probably cause an immediate complaint.

Tipping

In German restaurants the bill usually includes a tip. Whether an extra tip is given will depend on the quality of the service that was provided.

Accommodation

Twin beds are far more common than double beds in Germany. In fact, double beds are sometimes referred to as *französische Betten* ('French beds') and are seen as rather interesting, even slightly erotic. As with many other visitors, it is best to check with German visitors before giving them rooms with double beds.

Germans may consider Australian pillows to be strangely small (theirs are double the size), and they may have a problem knowing what to do with two sheets because they usually have only one (bottom) sheet.

Smoking

Smoking is no longer as popular as it was in Germany, but, having asked permission, it is possible to smoke almost everywhere. Therefore, as with many other visiting groups, it is necessary to be very tactful about 'No-smoking' requirements. However, smoking while others are eating is considered impolite behaviour.

Malaysians

Cultural Values

Malaysia the nation

Formerly British colonies or protectorates for many years, the Malaysian Federation was formed in 1963. Singapore was originally part of the Federation, but left to become an independent state in 1965.

Malaysia is geographically divided into three parts: the Malayan Peninsula, Sabah and Sarawak. It is roughly the size of Japan, but, with a population of approximately 21 million, has a much lower population density.

Malaysia is a parliamentary democracy with a king as head of state.

Economic growth rates in Malaysia have been among the highest in the world, averaging in excess of 8 per cent per year in the first half of the 1990s. Malaysia has one of the highest standards of living in Asia. In one generation, Malaysia has moved from being a Third World commodity producer to become a rapidly developing manufacturing nation. While this has resulted in major social change, each of the ethnic groups has largely maintained its traditional cultural values.

Ethnic groupings

The Malays, together with the approximately 25 indigenous tribal groups in Sabah and Sarawak, constitute 60 per cent of the population. The Chinese constitute approximately 30 per cent of the population, and the Indians approximately 9 per cent.

To a very great extent, the information supplied about Chinese and Indians in other sections of this book holds true for those groups in Malaysia. There has been very little intermarriage, partly because of religious differences, and each group has remained culturally distinct. As Malays are the dominant group, this section will concentrate on the Malay culture in Malaysia. Malay culture and food is similar to that of Indonesia.

The *bumiputras*

The Muslim Malays (and the other indigenous groups in Sabah and Sarawak) are called *bumiputras* ('sons of the soil') to distinguish them from the Chinese and Indians, who were brought in by the British colonists as immigrant labour.

At the time of independence, the Malays lived mostly in the rural areas and were (socially and economically) the least advanced group, although educated Malays had helped in running the government bureaucracy. Since independence, the Malays comprise the majority of public servants who administer the country.

There has been a policy of affirmative action in favour of the bumiputras in a number of fields. For example, the bumiputras are allotted some stock ownership in certain public companies, and preference in school, university and government placements.

Chinese-Malaysians

Chinese-Malaysians accept the situation as described above because they have prospered. They dominate the economy and business, although in recent years there has been a push by the government to develop businesses run by the bumiputras.

Indian-Malaysians

The Indians form two economic groups: the larger (mainly Tamils) work as labourers in the rubber plantations, whereas the smaller (Indians from other regions and higher castes) work in the professions as teachers, doctors and lawyers.

Racial tensions

Racial tension between the Malays and Chinese has occurred in Malaysia. However, in recent years, there has been an attempt by the government to create a more genuinely Malaysian national identity, and to develop inter-communal harmony among the multi-ethnic population. Genuine partnerships between Malays and Chinese in business have been fostered, Chinese have been given more opportunities in higher education, and greater emphasis has been placed on English language proficiency. All these moves have been supported by non-Malays.

Nevertheless, there are still memories of the savage 1969 race riots, and some prejudices remain. Some Malays still see Chinese as greedy, lacking in courtesy, and ready to cheat them in business, while Chinese tend to regard Malays as too relaxed and dependent on the government.

Despite this, on a day-to-day basis, the different groups generally practise a 'live and let live' philosophy. The Malay cultural tradition (which values courtesy in social relations, restraint in expressing aggressive feelings, and hospitality to strangers) provides a foundation for this tolerance.

Religion

Islam is the official religion, but Malaysia is a secular state (not one run by Islamic law). Freedom of religion is guaranteed. Most Malays (and many of the other indigenous groups) are Muslims, but there are also indigenous Christians who are mainly centred in the eastern Malaysian states of Sabah and Sarawak.

The other two large ethnic groups have their own religions: most of the Indians are Hindus, and the Chinese are predominantly Buddhists.

The government tries to avoid offending Muslim sensibilities, whilst trying to prevent extreme, fundamentalist Muslims from forcing their beliefs on others. This Islamic fundamentalism is strongest in the northern states. In the state where these fanatical Muslims have control, public consumption of alcohol, and having sex outside marriage, are offences. The Buddhist, Hindu and Christian minorities are always afraid that this sort of fundamentalism may become dominant, and thus exclude them from the mainstream of society.

Courtesy and harmony valued

As Muslims, Malays observe the protocol of *budi* which is manifested in two ways.

▼ As individuals, Malays observe *adab*, which means showing courtesy to all people at all times.
▼ As members of society, they must observe *rukun* . This means acting in ways that encourage harmony in the family, the community and the whole society.

While the need for harmony is stressed, when this breaks down Malays can react quite violently. The expression 'to run amok' has been borrowed from Malay.

Fatalism and free will

The Malay expression *tidak apa* is similar to the Thai expression *mai pen rai*. It expresses a feeling of indifference to the ordinary tasks of daily life. However, in recent years, there has been less emphasis on accepting fate, and more on working hard to achieve material success.

The family

The family is the most important social unit. Extended families share housing where possible. Loyalty, co-operation with family members, and meeting obligations are all highly valued.

Western influences

As in many other societies, through the widespread influence of international television and other media, young people are becoming more exposed to Western values, and may behave differently from older generations.

Gender roles

While men remain dominant socially, economically and politically, the number of women in the workforce is growing, and women have achieved important positions in all areas (for example, the inclusion of female ministers in the Cabinet). Well-off women see no problem in combining home and career because servants are easily available.

Gift-giving

Giving gifts (*hadiah*) is an important part of Malay social and business life. The size or cost of the gift is less important than the emotion expressed through the gift.

As in other Asian cultures, it is customary not to open the gift in front of the giver (because this may give the impression that the gift is seen as more important than the person giving it).

Bribes and commissions

As in many other societies, the distinction between a bribe and a commission (often called a perquisite or 'perk') is not clear. It is best not to make any judgment until one understands exactly what is involved.

The same applies to practices which might, in Australia, be criticised as nepotism. In Malaysia, such practices are seen as 'looking after the family'.

Prayer-times

It should be remembered that, for Muslims, Friday afternoons represent an especially important holy prayer-time. On other days they are also required to pray five times during the day at fixed times in a mosque (or another appropriate place if a mosque is unavailable).

Language and Communication

Verbal Communication

Amongst Malays, a formal, softly spoken, indirect style of communication is generally valued.

The national language

Bahasa Malaysia (*Bahasa Melayu*) is the national language, and is understood in all areas of the country. It is similar to *Bahasa Indonesia*, but there are differences in vocabulary and grammar. People from both countries can be offended if this distinction is not recognised.

Other languages

English is learnt at school, and is widely spoken and understood (especially in commerce and industry).

Ethnic Chinese speak different Chinese dialects (including Mandarin, Cantonese, Hakka or Hokkien).

Tamil and Hindi are the main languages of the Indians.

Names and forms of address

Older people are introduced first, and women before men.

Malay names are similar to Indonesian names. The distinctive name of the person comes first. Most names are derived from Arabic.

If a Malay man is named *Ahmed bin Ali*, he is formally addressed as '*Encik Ahmed*'. Friends would call him '*Ahmed*'. The *Encik* means 'Mr', or can be translated as 'Sir'. The connective *bin* means 'son of' and is usually dropped. *Ali* is the father's name, not a surname. He would be addressed as '*Mr Ahmed Ali*' or '*Mr Ahmed*'.

A woman's name could be *Kemala binti* ('daughter of') *Rahman* (father's name). She would be addressed as '*Miss Kemala*'. If married to Mr Ahmed, she could be addressed as 'Mrs Kemala' or 'Mrs Kemala Ahmed'. Alternatively, she might be called *Puan* ('Mrs'), which can be translated as 'Madam'. Younger women can be addressed as *'Cik'*, although this has become rather outdated now that more women are working.

Titles

Titles are common, and should be used if possible.

Tunku and *Tengku* are comparable to 'Prince' and 'Princess'.

Tan, Tan-sri and *Dato* (or *Datu*) are, in descending order of status, the titles of high ranking male officials. *Toh Puan, Puan Sri* and *Datin* are the equivalents for their wives.

Muslims can be given the title *Hajji* (if a man) or *Hajjah* (if a woman) if they have made the pilgrimage to Mecca, and such people may wear special clothing (a man can wear a white cap, and a woman a white muslim veil or cap).

If in doubt about titles, it is best to use 'Sir' or 'Madam', or 'Mr', 'Mrs' or 'Miss' plus the first name.

Status and words for 'you'

In Bahasa Malaysia there are several equivalents for 'You'. These indicate a desire to be formal, informal, respectful or condescending. However, people may avoid using these words for 'You', and instead use titles. For example, they might ask 'Where is Sir from?' rather than 'Where are you from?'.

The importance of 'face'

The concept of 'face' is important for Malays. 'Face' is linked to self esteem, and this depends on how one is perceived by others.

If people lose 'face', they experience shame and humiliation. The force of public and social opinion is very strong, and what neighbours think is of great importance. Suicide is one extreme reaction to severe loss of 'face'.

Severe loss of 'face' can also cause the uncontrolled frenzy described as 'running amok'.

There are many potential sources of loss of 'face' for the individual, and for the groups to which they belong. These include:

▼ public reprimands or criticism;
▼ being the object of jokes or ridicule (even in a friendly way);
▼ being singled out; or
▼ being the subject of a public disagreement.

Because of the above, Australians should be careful of making monocultural judgments such as 'they can't take a joke' or 'they're touchy and unreasonable'.

A diplomatic incident

In 1994 Australians were surprised when there was such a strong, angry reaction in Malaysia to public criticism by the Australian Prime Minister (Mr Keating) of the Malaysian Prime Minister (Dr Mahathir).

With an understanding of Malay culture, it will be apparent that there were two issues here:

▼ the higher the status of the person publicly criticised, the greater the loss of 'face' for the group with which he or she is identified; and

▼ the Malay equivalent of the word 'recalcitrant' (which Mr Keating used to describe Dr Mahathir) has a much more negative meaning in that language (in a culture that values harmony), than does the English equivalent in Australian culture.

Non-Verbal Communication

Greetings

Shaking hands is common among men in all three Malaysian ethnic groups, especially when interacting with Westerners.

When interacting with women it is best to wait for them to initiate any contact.

Among themselves Malays often bow slightly, and may use the *salaam* gesture of greeting. This involves bringing the hands to the heart to signify 'I greet you from the heart'. To show respect, both hands are used when greeting people of higher status or older people.

Touching

As in all the Asian cultures studied in this book, public touching between the sexes is uncommon. For instance, public displays of affection in public between husband and wife are not usual.

In crowded areas people tend to keep their hands close to their body to show that touching others is not desired.

Significance of certain parts of the body

Among Malays and Indians it is very important to avoid touching the head as they believe it is sacred (because the soul or spirit resides there).

Showing the sole of the shoe or foot is disrespectful.

On most formal occasions, it is very rude to cross one's legs, and both feet should be kept flat on the floor.

As the left hand is used for washing after defaecating, and is considered unclean, it should not be used for eating, for passing things or for touching people.

These behaviours are common among South and South-East Asian cultures, but are not shared by those of East Asia such as the Japanese, Chinese and Koreans.

Other points to note

Some other points to note in dealing with Malaysians include the following:

▼ It is impolite to clear the throat, or to blow the nose in a very public way, especially during meals.
▼ As with Indians, Chinese and other Asian cultures, it is rude amongst Malays to use one finger to beckon with, or point at, a person. The whole hand is used (with a gesture similar to waving) to mean 'Come here'.
▼ Standing with hands on hips suggests anger.
▼ It is best to avoid making a fist with one hand and hitting it against the other hand, because many Malays see this as an obscene gesture.

Dining, Service and Accommodation Preferences

Dining Preferences
Eating utensils

Malays eat with spoons, and use their right hand only. They may see knives as weapons.

It is acceptable to use a fork in the left hand to push food into the spoon in the right hand.

Food and drink laws

The fact that almost all Malays are Muslims influences their eating and drinking habits. Eating pork, eating meat that is not *halal*, and drinking alcohol, are *haram* ('forbidden').

Animals have to be slaughtered in a special way to make meat halal, (that is, fit for Muslim consumption). All beef and mutton sold in Malaysia is halal, and so is most packaged, frozen chicken.

It is not tactful to suggest meeting a Malay in a bar for a drink. However, some do drink alcohol, and they may argue that it is not the alcohol itself which is forbidden, but the act of becoming intoxicated.

The fasting month of Ramadan is strictly observed. People fast from sunrise to sunset.

Smoking, and the touching of dogs (which are considered unclean) are *makruh* (which means that they are allowed, but not encouraged).

Malaysian cuisine

Rice is the main food in a Malay meal.

As in Indonesia and Thailand, long grains (cooked without salt to be dry and separate) are preferred to the short-grained varieties more common in Japan and Korea.

Malay food is hot and spicy. Small bowls of cut chillies in vinegar, soy sauce and the *sambal* (a mixture of garlic, chilli and ginger) are placed on the table for guests to add to their food. Malays appreciate the provision on the table of similar tasty sauces (where appropriate) in Australian restaurants.

Unlike many other Asian cultures (where desserts are not often served), Malays enjoy rich, sweet desserts. These are often based on sago, glutinous rice, mung beans or bean flour. In some recipes sweet spices such as cardomon, cinnamon and cloves are used. Palm sugar adds sweetness, pandamus leaf (the Asian equivalent of vanilla bean) adds flavour, and coconut milk provides added richness.

Drinks

A range of drinks (including tea, coffee, juices and soft drinks) should be available, and alcohol should not be offered immediately.

Service and Accommodation Preferences

Availability of staff

All reasonably well-off Malaysians are used to having servants in their homes, and to having people waiting on them. Hotels and restaurants in Malaysia have large numbers of staff who are trained to be very attentive.

Dress

As with Indonesians, Malaysians (especially Muslim Malays and traditional Hindus), disapprove of dress that is too brightly coloured or informal, especially if a lot of bare skin is shown.

While few Malay women wear a veil, some do wear head scarves or other headwear in the style associated with their religion.

Orientation of rooms

Malaysian hotels have a small arrow on the ceiling indicating the direction of the holy city of Mecca. Muslims face towards Mecca when they pray. For this reason, Muslim guests may ask about the direction of their room or the hotel.

Personal hygiene

In Malay homes, the toilet is separate from the bathroom, and in rural areas and smaller hotels and restaurants the squat type of toilet is common. In top hotels, in addition to toilet paper, there is a small hose on the wall to use for bodily hygiene. In other public toilets, there is a bucket of water.

In all but modern hotels there is a three-foot-high bath. People stand next to this, fill a scoop or water dipper with water, and splash it over themselves. The bath acts as a catch-basin. If it gets too full, water is scooped from it. There is no need to keep the floor dry.

Tipping

Tipping is becoming widespread. A 15 per cent service charge and tax is added to all bills. Taxi drivers, porters and bellboys all expect to be tipped.

 # Indians

Cultural Values

India today

The Republic of India gained independence from Britain in 1947, and is the world's most populous democracy. India has a population of more than 900 million. The population of India increases each year by a number equivalent to the current Australian population.

India has experienced rapid economic growth in recent years and is fast becoming a major economic power. There are extremes of poverty and wealth, with about 30 per cent of the population in poverty, and a wealthy upper class of several million people. The increasingly wealthy middle class is expected to grow rapidly in coming years.

There are also substantial populations of Indian origin living in many other countries, for example, in Malaysia, Singapore and Fiji.

Languages and cultural variety

Linguistically and culturally, India is more like a continent than an ordinary country. The different parts of India have different histories, languages, customs and cuisine. There is as much cultural variety within India as there is in the whole of Europe.

As with other societies, the introduction of satellite television throughout India has meant that modern Western ideas have significantly influenced many aspects of life, making material prosperity more desirable, and contributing to changes in cultural values and traditions. However, 70 per cent of the population still lives in rural areas, and even highly educated people tend to remain conservative and to retain their traditions in these areas.

It is difficult to generalise about values and customs because there are important differences between the north and south, as well as significant differences within each region, within each religious group, and within each social class. Furthermore, religion and language separate people far more than do ethnic background or geography.

Religion in India

Religious life forms the central theme of the nation. The majority of Indians are Hindus (approximately 83 per cent of the population), with Muslims making up approximately 12 per cent, Christians and Sikhs approximately 2 per cent each, and Buddhists approximately 1 per cent.

With such a large overall population, even small percentages constitute large numbers of people.

The influence of Hinduism

The minority groups actively resist losing their identity and becoming part of the Hindu majority. Nevertheless, Hindu philosophy and traditions are a fundamental part of Indian society.

One example is the belief in reincarnation. The birth of people into particular positions in life is thought to be determined by the balance of the right and wrong actions of their souls through their previous life-cycle. This belief also leads to people making religious rituals very much part of their daily life (even if they otherwise indulge in all sorts of vices), because religious rituals determine their progress through the cycle of life and death. The belief that one's life is determined at birth (and that everything that happens is one's *karma*) permeates most aspects of life, including attitudes to work.

The caste system

In the section on *Hinduism* earlier in this book we noted that Indian society is divided into hundreds of separate castes or sub-castes, each with its own status in society (*see Important Religions & Philosophies: Hinduism for more detail*).

The traditional Hindu belief was that an individual is born into a particular caste as a result of karma earned in a previous life. Caste was therefore accepted by almost all Hindus as part of the natural order of things. This is no longer so.

Adverse discrimination based on caste is now illegal and education is helping to break down caste barriers. Caste no longer determines occupation, although most well-educated and wealthy Indians still come from the

Birla Temple, New Delhi

higher castes, and most of the dirtiest and most menial tasks are still performed by people from the lowest castes.

Since independence, and because India is a democracy and their votes are valuable, the lowest group, the Untouchables or *Dalits*, have been able to use their numbers to improve their conditions in some respects. For example, they are now guaranteed a fixed percentage of government jobs. However, these and similar government initiatives have been resented by some Hindus from the higher castes, and violations of caste norms (for example intermarriage with other castes) can still cause fierce, violent reactions.

An hierarchical society

As a result of these beliefs, an hierarchical organisation of society, the workplace and the family is generally accepted. A son should obey his father and support him in old age, and a superior is expected to behave in an autocratic (but paternal) manner, whereas a subordinate should be compliant and respectful like a son.

There is great respect for elders. All Indian languages have respectful terms for each older family member. As in many other Asian cultures, members of the younger generation call older Indians 'aunt' and 'uncle' to show respect and affection, even when they are not related.

The family

The migration of many people to the cities and towns in search of economic opportunity has helped weaken many traditions, including that of extended families. Nevertheless, outside the big cities, the majority of Indians still live in an extended family, in which brothers remain together after marriage and bring their wives into the parental household.

The concept of *dharma* (which includes ideas of duty and social harmony) is important in India, and is typical of a collectivist society in the way it stresses the interdependence of the 'in-group'. The identity and worth of an individual is closely linked with his family's reputation.

In general, children are not encouraged to be self-reliant, and the family makes the decisions that affect an individual's future. For example, the family provides the connections needed to get a job or other favours. As a result, the character of the respective families is crucial when marriage proposals are being considered. Arranged marriages are still the norm, and divorce is considered a social disgrace.

A collectivist society

The strong sense of mutual interdependence in the family is reflected in the collectivist nature of society as a whole.

Most organisations have many overlapping 'in-groups' which co-operate and make sacrifices for the common good, and often protect members of the group. Relatives, caste members, and people sharing a language or religion may form 'in-groups'. Within these groups, people are quite informal, visit one another readily, and stay for meals without a formal invitation.

The high value placed on the group, especially the family or *jati*, leads to the prevalence of behaviour that would be viewed in Western countries as nepotism and corruption.

Gender roles

By tradition, Hindu women have not been treated as the equals of men. However, more recently, women have had access to education, and some have been remarkably successful in a number of fields, including the professions, business and politics. The former Prime Minister, Indira Gandhi, for example, was one of the first women in the world to become leader of an important nation.

The status of women varies according to their class, with middle-class women more likely to be treated as equals by their husbands, especially if they work outside the home.

The preference for a son is still widespread as a son guarantees that the family will continue. In addition, a son performs the last rites after his parent's death.

Daughters, on the other hand, can mean huge expense. This is because, in many cases, a large part of the family's income has to be spent on a marriage dowry. This continues despite its being illegal (although many educated Indians are giving up the practice). The size of the dowry can decide how well or badly a woman is treated in her husband's home.

Females also continue to suffer from practices such as female infanticide, child marriage (both of which are, of course, against the law) and *purdah* (being secluded in the house).

Language and Communication

Verbal Communication

Languages

There are at least 300 languages in India, with 24 having one million speakers or more.

In 1947 Hindi was made the official language because it is by far the most commonly spoken of all the Indian languages and is the first language of about 40 per cent of the population. There are now 19 official languages, including English, which is also widely spoken because of the long period of British rule. In fact, English is often the language of national communication, especially in education, business and the courts.

Indian English does differ from British English in grammar and vocabulary (much more than does Australian English). Indian English differs even more in accents and intonation patterns because these are influenced by native languages. Indian English can be hard to understand at first (just as many people have difficulty with the Australian accent).

Names

As a general rule, people's names provide information about the caste to which they belong, and the region of the country from which their family comes. For example, the family name Gupta comes from the trading class, although many have now gone into the professions.

There are different regional and religious naming systems.

All male Sikhs have the name Singh (meaning 'lion'), either preceding their family name, or as their family name, whereas females all have the name Kaur. Alternatively, they merely use initials and family name.

Indians from the north (including Hindi, Gujerati and Bengali speakers) have a given name, their father's name, and a family name. Indians from the south (including Tamil, Malayalam, Telugu and Kannada speakers) have their father's given name, followed by their own given name.

It is advisable always to address people by a title such as 'Mr' or 'Mrs', followed by the last name.

Greetings

The traditional greeting is the *namaste* (both palms together at chest level as if in prayer, together with a slight bow or nod of the head). In larger cities, handshakes are becoming more common for men, but are still unusual for women. The namaste is also used when saying goodbye.

Business cards are exchanged at the first meeting, although not always at the beginning.

Some other points

Some other points to note include the following:

▼ It is customary to engage in small talk before getting down to business. To succeed in business ventures, it is is vital to work at building relationships.
▼ Punctuality is not usually as important as is the building of relationships.
▼ Individuals do not generally take responsibility for errors although subordinates may be blamed. Only the top person makes decisions in most situations.
▼ Older, less 'Westernised' Indians may avoid saying 'No' directly, and prefer to avoid giving negative news.

Non-Verbal Communication

Showing emotion

Most Indians smile less often than the people of some other Asian cultures, and tend to smile only when they are happy or in a pleasant situation.

In general, emotions are shown rather than hidden. Ideally, anger should not be overt, but it may be displayed by a superior to an inferior. It is polite to be softly spoken.

Touching

Indian culture is similar to all other Asian cultures in that men and women do not usually touch one another in public, and public displays of affection are not considered proper even between married couples.

Significance of certain parts of the body

As with South Asian and South-East Asian cultures, the feet are considered to be the dirtiest part of the body, and feet or soles of shoes should not touch anyone, be pointed at people, or be put on furniture.

The head is considered a sacred part of the body and should not be touched.

Using the left hand is avoided in many situations because it is the unclean hand.

Other gestures

Pointing and beckoning are done with the whole hand, rather than with one finger. Beckoning a waiter is done in different ways. In some parts of India it is the custom to snap the fingers and perhaps hiss.

Indians sometimes move their head from side-to-side. This can mean that they merely hear the speaker, or it may indicate agreement. Indirect questions may be needed to check the exact meaning.

Dining and Service Preferences

Dining Preferences

Eating utensils

Food is traditionally eaten with the fingers of the right hand. The left hand is thought to be unclean and is never used to pass or accept food. Some orthodox Hindus think that spoons, forks and plates which are used again and again are unhygienic, but, in most cities, Western customs have taken over, and dinner plates, forks and spoons are used.

Indian cuisine

Common features of northern Indian cuisine are wheat flour *chapati*, lamb, *ghee* and yogurt.

In the south, rice replaces wheat, and ingredients such as coconut, mustard seeds and hot chillis are common. Cream, milk and cheese are used as ingredients in sweets, as well as curries.

Fluffy, dry rice is preferred. Long, thin grains are thought to be best, and rice must be cooked with salt.

Food laws

Hindus generally do not eat beef because the cow is considered sacred. Some traditional, high-caste Hindus may follow quite strict dietary rules, and may not eat any meat products at all.

Indeed, many Indians are vegetarian. Some will not eat even eggs or fish.

Muslims, generally, should not eat pork or drink alcohol, and may eat meat killed only in the correct way.

Drinks

Alcohol is not commonly served with meals.

Cold water has been the traditional accompaniment to food, but many Indians prefer sweet drinks such as sherbet or lemonade.

Men who drink alcohol tend to prefer a hard drink (usually Scotch and soda), although some drink beer. More women are beginning to drink alcohol. In recent years, India has begun to make its own wines, but most Indians are not familiar with wine. Some Indians use the word 'wine' to refer to any kind of alcohol.

Service Preferences

Availability of staff

Most Indians who travel overseas are used to having servants in their homes and to there being numerous servants and waiters in any hotel or restaurant which they frequent. They would therefore be used to having people immediately available, and deferential, to meet their slightest wish.

Clothing and personal appearance

Very informal clothing is frowned upon. In the cities, Indian men usually wear Western clothes to the office but often relax in loose-fitting traditional dress at home. Most Indian women wear saris or *salwar-kameez* (a long shirt over baggy trousers gathered at the ankle).

A *tika* (dot) in the middle of the forehead symbolises a blessing from the gods. It can have religious (or caste) significance, but is nowadays often merely a part of women's fashion.

Tipping

Tipping is common in India. Most large hotels and good restaurants add a 10 per cent service charge, and porters and taxi drivers expect a tip.

▼ Questions

••••••••••••••••••••••••••••••••••••••

Japanese

1 Japanese visitors are important to the Australian tourist industry because they comprise almost a quarter of all overseas visitors. However, they are critical of three aspects of this industry. What three aspects?

2 Australia is sometimes described as an especially egalitarian country in which 'Jack thinks he is as good as his master', and where people call almost everyone by their first name. How does Japan differ in this respect?

3 Read the following description of events at a large American hotel, and then answer the questions below.

> At the beginning of a cross-cultural training program, employees at the New York *Sheraton Hotel* were asked to write down their impressions of the Japanese they served. One waitress commented: 'Sometimes they leave their food untouched. I remember one fellow who just stared at his eggs, and poked them around with his fork. When I asked him if there was anything wrong, he said, 'No'. But I noticed his eggs looked a little runny, so I offered to take them back and get some cooked longer. He started thanking me, and, when I brought him better cooked eggs, he ate every last bite. Why don't they just complain or something?' Other training staff frequently commented: 'the Japanese are always happy; they smile a lot'.
> (Shames & Glover, 1989)

If you were supervising staff who made similar comments, what key things would you tell them about Japanese behaviour and communication-style? In particular:

a Why don't Japanese visitors complain if something is wrong?

b Why are they so grateful if their needs are anticipated?

c Why do smiles not always mean they are happy and satisfied?

4 If you needed to apologise to a Japanese guest for something which was the fault of your hotel or travel service, what might you say and do to best satisfy your guest?

5 If you saw Japanese guests getting very drunk and arguing, how would you judge it from an intercultural point of view (that is, from the way it would be seen in Japanese culture), as opposed to a monocultural point of view (that is, the way you would judge it based on your own cultural values)?

6 Read the following description of an unsuccessful business lunch, and then answer the question below.

> An Australian executive in the hotel industry was hosting a lunch for two Japanese businessmen in the hope of doing business with them. At the beginning of their conversation the Australian scribbled notes on the back of the *meishi* (business cards) which the Japanese had given him, and then, just before sitting, he put the cards in his wallet in his back trouser-pocket. Soon after (because he had a cold), he blew his nose a number of times. The conversation became strained, and no real progress was made in the business dealings.

What two things do you think probably made the Japanese feel uncomfortable? Briefly explain your answer.

7 When telling Japanese visitors about Australian restaurants, why do they need to be told about making reservations, the opening hours and the 'BYO' system?

8 **a** Give three reasons explaining why it would be a good idea for restaurants (which cater for large numbers of Japanese) to provide attractively presented buffet-meals with lots of fresh and lightly cooked foods.

b What four services (apart from appropriate plate-food) would you ensure were available to provide greater enjoyment for your guests?

9 If you were seating and waiting on a group of Japanese visitors in which one man seemed older and more important than the others, what might you do?

10 Imagine that you have just taken over the management of a hotel and you want to attract more Japanese guests. Read the following facts about this rather old-fashioned, badly run Australian hotel, and then answer the questions below.

a Usually no-one greets any guests. They have to find the reception desk and say that they want to check-in.

b Guests are given a form on which they have to write quite a few details and sign their names.

c A porter/roomboy shows guests to their room, bringing their luggage sometime later. He may show them some of the facilities in the room, but they are left to find the folder which explains about room service, housekeeping etc. (in English).

d The roomboy hands the keys to the guests as he leaves, and expects a tip at this stage.

e Information about fire procedures is on the door in English.

f All the hotel bathrooms have showers only. One towel per guest per day is provided.

g The security is slack. There are no chains on the doors, and nowhere to store valuables in the room.

h Drycleaning and laundry are not returned until the following day.

i There is no drinking water in the refrigerator.

j Check-out is often slow, with a long wait for a porter to come to the room.

Having noted these hotel practices (and bearing in mind what you know about Japanese needs and expectations), outline what changes you would make to each of the above practices to achieve your aim of increasing the number of Japanese guests.

Thais

1 Most Thais are Buddhists. What belief in this religion has led to the tendency to think that one's present wellbeing is more important than one's future career prospects?

2 If you had Thai staff members working under you, what might they expect from you, and why might it be inadvisable to treat them in a critical or unkind manner?

3 Why has Thai behaviour been likened to a rubber band that is usually loose, but is sometimes stretched very tight?

4 **a** What are two questions that are polite for Thais to ask but seem too personal and inquisitive in English-speaking cultures?

   b Why do Thais ask these kind of questions?

5 How do you think Thai visitors would judge a manager or supervisor who became angry and publicly criticised a staff member?

6 If you were waiting on Thai guests and they smiled whenever you did something for them, and waved to you when you were in another part of the restaurant, how would you interpret this behaviour?

7 When interacting with Thais, what would you need to be careful not to touch or reach across?

8 A Thai woman who was married to an Australian went to the funeral of a relative of her husband in Australia. Her husband's family were shocked because she smiled quite often during the funeral. Why do you think this cultural clash occurred?

9 A waiter in Australia found that if he avoided passing things to Thai visitors with his left hand they gave him a bigger tip. Why do you think this happened?

10 If you could not offer Asian food to Thai guests, what type of Western food might you offer to appeal to them?

Americans

1 Although there are many faiths in the USA, it remains a predominantly Protestant (Christian) society. What is meant by the term 'the Protestant work ethic', and how is it reflected in American society?

2 What do the very different numbers of lawyers in the USA and Japan show about the cultural values in these two societies?

3 Read the following account of difficulties between an American supervisor and an Australian staff member, and then answer the question below.

> An American from a large USA hotel chain and an Australian from one of the company's Australian hotels were sent to Hanoi to open a new hotel. The American was put in charge. After a short time, serious tensions developed between the two. The American felt that the Australian was slack, unco-operative and reluctant to take orders, while the Australian complained that the American was too critical and bossy.

What are three possible explanations for these not uncommon cultural misunderstandings?

4 If a visitor from the USA was having difficulty in understanding an Australian speaker, what might be three possible reasons?

5 When looking after American visitors, what would be important to remember about the following items:

a iced water?

b detailed orders?

c requests for information?

6 Differences exist between American idiom and Australian idiom. Read the following list of queries raised by an American visitor and then answer the questions below.

The American visitor asked:

i 'What is on the menu for *appetisers* today?'

ii 'What is on the menu for *entrée* today?'

iii 'We need a fresh *diaper* for the baby; can the hotel supply one?'

iv 'Could you bring a fresh *napkin* ?'

v 'Where is the nearest *drugstore* to this hotel?'

a What would you understand these queries to be (replacing the American idiomatic expressions with equivalent Australian terms)?

b Would you correct the American visitor's use of language and repeat the question back to him using Australian idiom?

7 What are the two reasons why USA visitors tend to expect a higher standard of service than do most Australians?

8 Why might some Australian service people see Americans as arrogant and rude?

9 What do you think might be the reason that surveys of American visitors to Australia show more satisfaction with Australian service now than used to be the case?

10 If you were running a hotel and wanted to attract more American guests, what three things would you do to achieve this aim?

Chinese

1 This century has seen a number of East Asian societies transformed from underdeveloped agricultural societies into industrialised, high-technology societies. Four of these societies have been called 'mini-dragons'.

a Name the three 'mini-dragons' that are predominantly Chinese societies.

b Name the fourth 'mini-dragon' (that is, the only 'mini-dragon' which is not predominantly Chinese).

▼

2 Historically, Australia has captured only a very small percentage of the Asian tourist market. This situation is improving and numbers are growing fast, but what negative perceptions has Australia had to overcome (and will need to continue overcoming)?

   (*Note:* This question is discussed in the *Introduction*.)

3 If you heard a society described as a Confucian society, what would you know were its three core values?

4 In all Chinese societies, relationships are very important, but in mainland China (in particular) the way the society operates is based on *guan xi* connections. Explain what *guan xi* means.

5 Give two examples from the Chinese language that show the importance of the extended family.

6 Read the following account of cultural problems, and then answer the question below.

   A relatively new Chinese staff member in a gymnasium in an Australian hotel said to his supervisor: 'I have to take my sister to the airport tomorrow so I can't come to work'. The Australian supervisor was annoyed, believing this showed a lack of commitment to the job. The Chinese worker was surprised that the supervisor seemed so displeased.

   What are the different cultural values which caused this misunderstanding?

7 Read the following account of a misunderstanding, and then answer the question below.

   The Chinese chef at a big resort hotel in Australia was a specialist in Cantonese cuisine. He had been hired in Hong Kong and brought to Australia by this hotel. After a few weeks, the Australian manager asked him if he would vary the menu by adding some Beijing and Shanghai dishes. The chef replied that he had been trained in Cantonese cooking and this would be difficult for him. However, he would look into the possibility. A similar conversation took place sometime later, but, after six months, the chef was still cooking only Cantonese dishes. The Australian manager felt angry and let down that the chef had not kept his word.

   Having read the section on communication-style, what is your explanation for this misunderstanding? (In your answer, comment on the Chinese attitude to saving and losing 'face'.)

8 **a** What are examples of expressions often used by Australians which Chinese tend to see as unnecessary and insincere in service interactions, or interactions with family and friends?

   b How might this difference explain why Chinese are sometimes seen as rude by service staff in Australia?

   c What other reasons might there be for this possible perception of Chinese?

9 You have become a part-owner of a small hotel which is hoping to attract more Chinese visitors. Read the following account of practices you note occurring in this hotel, and then answer the questions below.

   a When a group of old and young Chinese visitors arrive, most of the young people are attended-to and settled in their rooms first, because their names are on the booking list in that order.

   b The evening meal consists of a first course of chilled creamed potato and onion soup, a main course of large, thick slices of cold, rare roast beef and salad, and a dessert of cheese-cake and cream.

   c There is a 15-minute wait between the serving of each course, but the bill is brought before the last course is finished.

   d The breakfast consists of cheese omelette, cereal and cold milk, buttered toast and coffee.

   What changes would you make regarding each of the practices noted above?

10 What could Australia promote about its food and wine to attract more Chinese visitors?

Indonesians

1 Why is it more difficult to make generalisations about Indonesians than is the case with other tourist groups (such as Koreans and Japanese for example)?

2 Read the following comments by a Western businessman regarding a meeting with an Indonesian hotel manager, and then answer the question below.

   'I don't know what they are on about! I thought these Indonesians were good business men, but they make appointments and never arrive on time. As a matter of fact, I waited almost an hour for a manager of a hotel last week. I gave him an expensive tie-pin from our company but he didn't even open the gift! All he seemed interested in was showing me his business card with his name and company position printed on it! (I was going to give him my card at the end of the meeting.) I did give him a file of our promotional material in Bahasa Melayu but he didn't seem very impressed with it, despite its costing us quite a few dollars to get it specially translated. He had to finish the meeting in a hurry (he murmured something about 'prayer time') and didn't want to meet at a bar to continue the transactions.'

How could you assist this man to improve his understanding of Indonesian customs, and thus improve his chances of business success in Indonesia?

3 Read the following report, and then answer the question below.

In an article in the 1993 Harvard Business Review, a prominent Indonesian, Julius Tahija, who had had a top job in the Caltex Oil Company, was reported as saying that if you ask Indonesians to do something, they reply with 'Perhaps' or 'Maybe'. He went on to say that a tentative answer is preferred because a direct 'Yes' or 'No' is immodest. In addition, he said that when Indonesians nod and say nothing, it means that they hear you, not that they agree, and when they say 'Y-e-e-e-s-s' it means that they question what you are saying and may have already decided it is unacceptable.

What problems and misunderstandings might arise if an Indonesian was communicating in this indirect style with an Australian used to a more direct style of communication?

4 An Indonesian guest was very upset after an encounter in an Australian restaurant. Which one of the following do you think would be the most probable cause? Briefly explain your answer.

a The Australian waiter smiled a lot in a genuinely warm way.

b The Australian tried to speak Indonesian (although he did not speak it well).

c The Australian beckoned to the Indonesian to come to the table and then passed things over his head, accidentally touching his head, and finally handed him an information pamphlet with his left hand.

5 In Australia it is acceptable for men and women to hold hands or walk arm-in-arm in public, but it is most unusual for people of the same sex to do this, especially men. How is it different in Indonesia?

6 Read the following report, and then answer the question below.

In an article in the Sydney Morning Herald of 4 November 1994, Mike Carlton wrote that he had once attended a cheerful barbecue given by an Australian ambassador in Jakarta where he stood next to two Indonesians who were prodding gloomily at a 'bleeding steak, a couple of charcoaled snags, a slurp of tomato sauce and a splodge of coleslaw'. Unaware that he spoke Bahasa Indonesia, their comments were that the food was 'disgusting' and 'raw cow' and 'truly a primitive cuisine'.

Remembering what you have read about Indonesian cuisine, and taking note of the sort of problems described in the above report, what advice would you give hotel restaurants catering for Indonesian guests? (Do not forget that tourists often want to try out the food of the country they are visiting, while at the same time they may find it difficult to do without their usual foods for too long.)

7 In first-class hotels in Asia, guests are offered a choice of Western and Asian breakfasts. What would you recommend that hotels of a similar standard include in their breakfast menus for Indonesian visitors?

8 An Australian hotel was asked to prepare a dinner for a group of Indonesian visitors and were told not to include pork in the menu. When the main course (fillet steak) appeared, there was a small piece of bacon on the top of each piece of steak. What does this show about the cultural awareness of the staff involved, and what would you advise them?

9 If one accepts the view that the best experience for overseas tourists is to let them experience the unique and interesting aspects of the local culture (while consciously avoiding aspects that might upset or embarrass them), what aspects of Australian behaviour do you think might most upset or embarrass an Indonesian visitor?

10 There is a famous saying: 'When in Rome, do as the Romans do'. Indonesians have a similar saying: 'When in the buffalo's pen say 'lo' and when in the goat pen say 'baba'. Why might it not always be possible for Indonesian tourists in Australia to follow this advice?

South Koreans

1 Why is South Korea such an important tourist market for Australia?
2 a Remembering the history of Korea and its geographical position, why is it important to be able to distinguish Koreans from their neighbours, the Japanese and Chinese?
  b How might the family name help you do this?

3 How is the strength of the Confucian tradition in South Korea reflected in their attitude towards education?

4 If, in the course of your career, you need to do business with Koreans, how would you go about it? (In your answer, mention such matters as introductions, building up a relationship, socialising and business cards.)

5 If a Korean guest lost his temper and showed anger openly because of poor service, would this probably mean:

   a that he was merely letting off steam and was not particularly dissatisfied; or

   b that he was extremely upset and you would need to take it very seriously?

   Give a reason for your answer.

6 Read the following report, and then answer the question below.

> When Black Americans rioted in California, USA, they particularly targetted shops run by South Koreans to loot and vandalise. After these race riots, the Blacks were asked why this had happened. They explained that it was because they believed the South Korean shopkeepers acted as if they were superior because they did not smile or make friendly 'small talk' to them.

   From your reading about Korean communication, how would you explain this misunderstanding?

7 What body language might signal to you that a Korean guest had a negative reaction to something?

8 When you are interacting with people from other cultures it is important not to let your first reaction (usually a monocultural one) determine your interpretation of behaviour. Keeping this in mind, what conclusion would you reach if you saw a Korean man resting his hand on the thigh of another man, or holding hands with him?

9 What two types of food are of fundamental importance in Korean cuisine?

10 What would be useful to remember about the Korean view of getting drunk, singing and generally 'letting-go'?

Germans

1 Why has German society been compared to a symphonic orchestra? Explain briefly in your own words.

2 How do you think German visitors would probably view service staff who chatted in a friendly, informal way, made jokes, and gave rather vague, general answers when asked for information about places and times? Explain your answer by referring to German cultural values and communication-style.

3 Give examples that illustrate each of the following (one example for each):

  a the German emphasis on not disturbing others;

  b the German emphasis on privacy; and

  c the importance of rules and order in German society.

4 Germans tend to be more formal than Australians. Give one example related to communication that shows this.

5 Describe a gesture during conversation that is generally acceptable in Australia but is less acceptable to most Germans.

6 Which one of the following types of spoken communication causes problems when Germans translate directly into English:

  a requests;

  b refusals; or

  c compliments?

  Give an example.

7 Germans tend to be health conscious. How is this illustrated in relation to their dining habits?

8 A colleague with whom you are working in a restaurant says to you:

    'Germans love beer and sausages; all you need to do is give them lots of beer and sausages, and they will be happy.'

  How would you reply?

9 What is the usual German attitude towards time? How could this affect the type of service they expect?

10 At a restaurant in a big resort hotel in Australia, a group of German tourists were seen to call the waiter and loudly point out the dirty marks on two of their glasses. Why do you think this happened, and do you think it was unusual behaviour on their part?

Malaysians

1 **a** What are the three main ethnic groups in Malaysia?

  b Which is the dominant political group?

2 **a** To whom does the term *bumiputras* refer?

b Why does the Malaysian Government have a policy of positive discrimination in their favour?

3 If you saw the name *Tunku Razaleigh Hitam* on a list of overseas visitors, what would it tell you about the person's likely nationality, ethnic group, sex and status?

4 If you were good friends with a Malay colleague but you had a public disgreement with him at a meeting, should you be surprised if he was no longer friendly and appeared to you to be sulking? What might be the explanation?

5 Some aspects of non-verbal communication are common to a number of Asian ethnic groups. Which of the following groups consider the left hand to be unclean and also consider touching the head to be absolutely taboo? (There may be more than one correct answer.)
   a Indians?
   b Malays?
   c Chinese?

6 Why might Malays prefer the food served to them not to require cutting with a knife?

7 Although you might assume that a Malay visitor would probably not drink alcohol, could you be sure? Give a reason for your answer.

8 Rice is part of virtually every meal for Malays, as it is for most other Asian cultures. However, different cultures prefer different sorts of rice and different methods of cooking/presentation. Comment on these preferences as they apply to the following cultural groups: the Malays, the Thais, the Koreans, the Japanese and the Indonesians.

9 What is Ramadan, and what might you have to take into account if you were a supervisor of Muslim workers at this time?

10 What might some Malays find different about the style of bathrooms and toilets in Australia, and the way people bathe?

Indians

1 Why is India seen as a tourist market with a big potential?
2 **a** Why are many modern Western ideas now spreading in India (even in rural areas)?
   b What might be one important effect of this?
3 **a** What religion is most associated with Indian culture?

b How have the beliefs of this religion contributed to the development and maintenance of the hierarchical organisation of Indian society?

4 Explain the concept of *dharma* and its importance to Indian culture.

5 Why is there still a widespread preference for sons in Indian culture?

6 Many Indians have had all their education in English and speak it fluently. Why might there still be difficulties when they first communicate (in English) with Australians?

7 If you saw an Indian moving his/her head from side to side during a conversation, how would you interpret this gesture?

8 Indians, in general, share certain beliefs with Indonesians, Malays and Thais regarding particular parts of the human body. Which three parts of the body have this shared significance, and what are the shared beliefs regarding each of these parts of the body?

9 The majority of Indians are Hindus. How does this influence their food and beverage preferences?

10 To what type of service would most well-off Indians be accustomed?

 # Answers Guide

The answers provided below are intended only as a guide. Students' answers may vary from the following suggested answers in wording, length, emphasis and choice of examples.

Japanese

1 Japanese have been critical of the following aspects of the Australian tourist industry:
  a Australia has been regarded as too expensive;
  b the insistence on visas for short-term visitors has been criticised; and
  c there has been a perceived lack of variety in the types of accommodation available.
2 Japanese society differs from Australian society in that Japan tends to be an hierarchical society with status determined by factors such as sex, position and seniority. Those of inferior status defer to those of higher status. First names are rarely used.
3 American service staff might have difficulty in understanding the following Japanese customs:
  a Japanese seldom complain or directly criticise service because of the emphasis on avoiding any unpleasantness, and the value placed on *enryo* which discourages people from expressing opinions and preferences.
  b Japanese visitors are grateful if service staff can anticipate their needs and preferences, and guess what is wrong, because this is the style of service to which they are accustomed. It removes the need for them to express their needs and complaints directly.

c Japanese smiles might not be reflecting happiness, contentment or amusement (as smiles usually do in Western cultures). A Japanese smile may indicate a wider range of emotions, including negative ones.

4 If apologising to a Japanese guest, it would be best to apologise for the inconvenience caused, but not to make excuses. Where possible and appropriate, some compensatory action (such as a complimentary service or gift) would be more effective than a mere verbal apology.

5 In Japanese culture, getting drunk is more widely tolerated than in Australian culture. A very different type of behaviour is acceptable when drinking (as contrasted with sober Japanese behaviour), including complaining and arguing. What is said and done is forgotten when people are again sober.

6 The Japanese probably felt uncomfortable because:

a Business cards represent a person's 'face' and must therefore be treated with respect. Scribbling on them (and then practically sitting on them!) could be seen as being deliberately disrespectful and insulting.

b Blowing one's nose in public (especially in the close face-to-face proximity of a dinner table), and using a handkerchief to do so, would be seen as very impolite, even disgusting, behaviour.

7 In explaining about Australian restaurants, it should be remembered that Japanese are used to restaurants' being open until late, seven days a week. Reservations are usually unnecessary. The 'BYO' system is uncommon in Japan, and guests from that country may require an explanation.

8 a Japanese appreciate buffet-meals' being offered because Japanese generally prefer fresh, lightly cooked food, and buffet-meals provide an opportunity for them to:

    i see what they are getting;

    ii be served without delay; and

    iii get the desired size of serving (Australian servings often being too large).

b Four extra services appreciated by Japanese include:

    i Japanese soy sauce;

    ii iced water;

    iii toothpicks; and

    iv hot towels.

9   It would be advisable to allow an older and more important Japanese guest to choose his seat, and to sit down first because this would give him the opportunity to sit in the appropriate position in relation to his subordinates. It would also be advisable to serve him first. The concept of 'face' is very important in Japanese culture. Because an older man usually has a high status, he has more 'face' to lose, and he will be more intensely embarrassed if he appears not to have been treated with the respectful deference to which he is accustomed.

10 The following ideas would help attract Japanese guests to a hotel:

    a Where possible, Japanese guests should be greeted and farewelled by staff of appropriate status.

    b Where necessary, assistance in filling out forms should be provided if there is no tour-guide to do this.

    c Luggage should be delivered to the room before, with, or immediately after, the guest is taken to the room. Hotel staff should make sure guests know where to locate all information. Important information about hotel facilities, and local shopping, should be readily available in Japanese.

    d Keys could be handed over at the front desk in envelopes, and staff should be made aware of Japanese tipping practices.

    e Information about fire procedures in English might not be of much help in an emergency. Self-explanatory visual illustrations (or at least some Japanese translations) would be advisable. ·

    f If possible, some bathrooms should be modified to include a bath; and a plentiful supply of towels should be provided.

    g Security should be upgraded. All rooms should have chains on the doors, and guests should be told where safes are located, and advised to use them.

    h Where stays are very short, arrangements for fast laundry and drycleaning services should be instituted.

    i Clean drinking water should be constantly available (and clearly indicated) in room refrigerators.

    j Check-out (and check-in) procedures should be as speedy as possible.

Thais

1 Because of their belief in reincarnation, many Thais tend to believe that economic status is the result of *karma* earned, or accumulated, in past

lives. Therefore, they see it as more important to concern themselves with their present wellbeing than with apparently pointless striving for a higher position.

2 Thai staff members working in Australia might expect protection and assistance, both at work and in their private lives. They could view critical or unkind treatment from a superior as extremely bad manners, or even as a deliberate attempt to humiliate them. They might react in a way that seemed extreme (to an Australian) because their feeling of *krenja* had changed to *krengklua*.

3 In comparison with Americans, Thais usually seem very easygoing and relaxed, even at work. However, when interacting with someone of a higher status, this changes and behaviour becomes more rigidly formal than anything comparable in America.

4 a 'How old are you?' and 'How much do you earn?' are two questions which appear intrusive to Westerners, but acceptable to Thais.

  b These questions are acceptable to Thais because it is necessary to quickly establish who has the higher status (and must, therefore, be treated more politely).

5 Thai visitors would probably view a critical supervisor as being crude, ignorant and immature. They might well view this behaviour as being more reprehensible than the inefficiency of the staff member (which drew the criticism in the first place).

6 These Thai gestures to an Australian waiter should be interpreted as follows:

  a smiles in this situation should be interpreted as a verbal 'thank you'; and

  b the waving gesture could well mean 'come here'.

7 Care should be taken to avoid touching (or reaching across) the heads of Thai visitors.

8 For a Thai woman at a funeral in her home society, it would have been considered polite and considerate to smile and to hide sorrow. In Western cultures people usually look serious or sad, and even cry openly at funerals.

9 There is a belief amongst Thais that the left hand is unclean, so the Thais appreciated the waiter's courtesy in passing things with his right hand only.

10 Vegetarian dishes, or dishes containing small pieces of meat in a spicy, tasty sauce, would appeal to Thai visitors if Asian food was unavailable. Rice could be offered as an alternative to potatoes or pasta.

▼

Americans

1 Protestantism is a form of Christianity that places great emphasis on the personal relationship between an individual and God (through Jesus Christ). The term 'Protestant work ethic' refers to the belief that every individual has a personal responsibility to God to work hard and make the most of their individual life. American society places great emphasis on the individual person, individual freedom and individual effort in all aspects of life and work.

2 The different numbers of lawyers in America and Japan may reflect different cultural values. In the United States fixing blame on an individual is important, whereas in Japan it is important to maintain harmony, and to work things out, in order to avoid publicly blaming an individual.

3 American and Australian views on service staff differ in the following ways:

a Americans tend to be more exacting about standards of performance;

b Australians generally prefer a more relaxed, informal style of interaction in the workplace; and

c Americans expect respectful deference if they have a higher position in the workplace, whereas Australians tend to respect (and work well for) only those whom they consider to have acceptable personal qualities.

4 An American visitor might have difficulty understanding an Australian because of the American's unfamiliarity with Australian accent, slang or idiom. The American might thus have difficulties with:

a the Australian accent; and/or

b the use of Australian (or British) slang; and/or

c the use of words not found in American English, or the use of familair words with a different meaning, or the pronouncing of words differently from the American pronunciation.

Australian service staff should be aware of all of these potential problems.

5 Many Americans expect:

a to be served iced water as soon as they sit down in a restaurant;

b any very detailed orders they give to be fulfilled exactly;

c staff quickly to find the answer if they cannot provide the required information immediately themselves.

6 **a** Because of the differences between American idiom and Australian idiom, you would understand (in Australian terms) the American's queries to be as follows:

    i 'What is on the menu for *entrée* today?'

    ii 'What is on the menu for *the main course* today?'

    iii 'We need a fresh *nappy* for the baby; can the hotel supply one?'

    iv 'Could you bring a fresh *serviette*?'

    v 'Where is the nearest *chemist shop* (or *pharmacist*) to this hotel?'

  b As a culturally sensitive staff member, you would not correct the American visitor, but would mentally 'translate' the question (to yourself only) and then answer the question immediately and accurately, or find out the exact answer as quickly as possible.

7 American visitors might expect a higher standard of service because:

  a Americans tend to stress high standards more than do people from other English-speaking countries; and

  b service in the United States is very competitive and efficient because staff depend on the tips they receive.

8 Australian service staff might perceive Americans as being arrogant because Americans tend to treat service staff in a more impersonal way (that is, as professionals who are being paid to do their job), whereas Australians tend to treat staff more as individuals (and therefore interact with them in a more personal way).

9 There has been a much greater emphasis on training and professionalism in the hospitality industry in Australia in recent years. As a result, Australian service is now more likely to meet American expectations. Courses in cross-cultural communication will also help in this process.

10 To help attract more American guests:

  a train staff to appreciate and understand American expectations;

  b provide staff with the awareness and skills to deal with possible communication and interpersonal problems (while maintaining their own Australian style); and

  c provide those services which Americans see as particularly important (for example, getting exactly what they order).

▼

Chinese

1 a Singapore, Hong Kong and Taiwan are the three predominantly Chinese economies which are known as 'mini-dragons'.

   b The fourth 'mini-dragon' is South Korea (and the only one which is not predominantly Chinese).

2 Negative perceptions of Australia in Asia include:

   a the tendency of the Asian press to feature any Australian news suggesting racism and/or criticism of Asian governments; and

   b the perception of Australia as an empty land with little but kangaroos (which reduces the 'status' of Australia as a desirable tourist destination).

3 The core values of a Confucian society are:

   a the importance of belonging to groups (the extended family, the clan and the state), and being loyal to this group;

   b the importance of harmony and good relationships within the group, with the young deferring to the old, and women deferring to their father, husband and sons; and

   c the importance of hard work and education (because it is believed that anyone can rise to the top through education).

4 The term *guan xi* means working to build up relationships and connections (through giving and returning favours), and then using these to get things done. In China it is difficult to do anything (for example, getting a child into a good school) without working through such connections.

5 The Chinese language reflects the importance of the extended family by:

   a the large number of kinship terms (for example, 16 names for aunt and uncle); and

   b the family name coming first, the given name for each generation, traditionally, coming second (thus placing people in the family chain), and the individual name coming last.

6 Cultural differences explain the contrasting values placed upon commitment to the job on the one hand, and commitment to the family on the other. The Chinese staff member placed the family first, whereas the Australian supervisor felt that work commitments should take precedence, except in very special situations.

7 Because of the predominant value placed on harmony and saving 'face', Chinese may avoid saying 'No' directly. A direct refusal means loss of 'face' especially for the person making the request. The chef probably thought the manager would realise that his unenthusiastic reply was

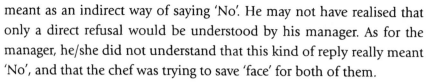

meant as an indirect way of saying 'No'. He may not have realised that only a direct refusal would be understood by his manager. As for the manager, he/she did not understand that this kind of reply really meant 'No', and that the chef was trying to save 'face' for both of them.

8 **a** Repeated use of 'Please', 'Thank you' and 'I'm sorry' are examples of expressions which Chinese might perceive as being insincere or unnecessary.

b Australians expect people to say these words automatically (even in the most routine interactions), and failure by Chinese to use them in this way might seem rude to Australians.

c Other reasons for Chinese appearing rude (to Australian observers) might be:

   i Chinese have an hierarchical view of society, and therefore they might see service staff as of lower status;

   ii Chinese might not bother being friendly to anyone who is not part of one of their 'in-groups'.

9 In an attempt to attract more Chinese visitors to the hotel:

a Attend to the older people first because this would probably be pre-ferred by both old and young people in a culture that defers to age.

b Avoid serving cold, cream-based, and cheese-based food, and large pieces of meat. Replace them with hot dishes featuring fish, vegetables or small pieces of meat in a tasty sauce. Provide rice and Chinese soy or chilli sauce as accompaniments for conservative eaters.

c Avoid long waits between courses because Chinese do not usually linger over meals. However, bringing the bill too quickly is not 'the done thing', and this should be delayed until it is requested.

d Avoid a breakfast menu containing mainly dairy foods because this is not received well by many Chinese. Provide alternatives which might be more acceptable (especially to those missing their customary breakfasts). Examples include green tea and at least one Chinese-type breakfast dish (such as Chinese porridge or noodles).

10 To attract more Chinese vistors, Australians could promote the fact that there are many good Chinese restaurants in Australia, and that they are cheaper than in some Asian cities. The new cuisine, a mixture of Asian and Western styles using excellent Australian ingredients, could also be pro-moted, as could our good quality wines which sell much more cheaply here than overseas.

▼

Indonesians

1 In view of the many different ethnic groups, and differences in language, religion and culture in Indonesia it is particularly difficult to generalise about Indonesian culture. For example, there are more than 500 languages and regional dialects spoken in Indonesia, and more than 300 ethnic groups. Although most Indonesians are Muslims, Indonesia is not an Islamic state, and there are substantial numbers of Christians, Hindus and Buddhists. The rapid changes brought about by modernisation in Indonesia add to the difficulty in making generalisation. The predominant culture is that of the Javanese, and Indonesian culture can be said to be part of the South-East Asian cultural tradition which is distinct from the dominant northern cultures of the region such as India and China.

2 To help this Western man improve his understanding of Indonesian customs, and hence improve his chances of doing business in Indonesia, the following should be explained:

   a Indonesians have a more relaxed attitude to time;

   b gifts are not usually opened in front of the giver (because it is seen as greedy and concentrating on the gift rather than the giver);

   c exchanging business cards at the outset is seen as very important;

   d it is insulting to give an Indonesian promotional material in the language of another country (Malaysia); although the languages are similar, they do have differences in vocabulary and grammar;

   e most Indonesians are Muslims, many of whom take very seriously their obligation to pray regularly at set times; and

   f many Indonesians do not drink alcohol; therefore, the suggestion of a bar as the meeting place might not be tactful.

3 In the direct communication-style which predominates in Australia:

   a People are expected to say 'Yes' or 'No' directly to a request (rather than 'Perhaps' or 'Maybe' as in Indonesia).

   b When people nod the head, this generally signals agreement (not merely that they are hearing, as this gesture may suggest in Indonesia).

   c If Australians say 'Y-e-e-e-s', it probably means hesitant or reluctant agreement (not a probable refusal, as in Indonesia).

4 Alternative c would be the cause of the upset because all of the following are unacceptable to Indonesians:

   i the beckoning gesture;

    ii touching someone's head; and

    iii passing things with the left hand.

In contrast, the other alternatives (smiling and trying to speak Indonesian) would be welcomed.

5 Indonesian customs regarding touching people in public are different from Australian customs. In Indonesia, public touching of a person of the opposite gender is frowned upon, but people of the same sex, especially men, often show friendship by touching (for example, by holding hands).

6 Hotel restaurants catering for Indonesian guests should consider the following:

    a offering at least one Asian-style dish on the menu;

    b offering dishes typical of the 'new cuisine' (which is basically a blend of Western and Asian styles and ingredients);

    c offering the choice of rice as an accompaniment; and

    d offering some Western dishes that do not include large pieces of rare meat.

7 Hotel breakfast menus for Indonesian visitors should include:

    a a choice of the best seasonal Australian fruits;

    b a savoury omelette;

    c a meat or noodles dish typically eaten in Indonesia at breakfast.

8 To serve Indonesian visitors bacon pieces on top of each piece of steak shows a complete lack of cultural awareness. The bacon would 'pollute' the steak, especially if it were cooked on top of the meat. Not only Muslims, but also some other Indonesians, do not eat pork, and could find it offensive, even disgusting, to be served pork in this way.

9 Embarrassing aspects of Australian culture (from an Indonesian perspective) might include:

    a the use of the left hand to pass food, and for other ordinary purposes;

    b public displays of physical affection between scantily clad people of the opposite sex (for example, in parks and on beaches).

10 Some of their strongest religious and cultural values would prevent Indonesians from participating in some very normal, popular Australian past-times (such as activities centred around alcohol and the eating of non-*halal* meat). Furthermore, tourists may not know what the local customs are. Much that is culturally determined is taken for granted, and people do not realise that their way of doing things is not universal. This applies to visitors to Australia as well as service personnel who are attending to these visitors. Misunderstandings can occur on both sides.

▼

South Koreans

1 South Korean visitors to Australia represent one of Australia's fastest growing source markets, and there is a huge potential for growth. Only a small percentage of South Korean overseas travellers come to Australia at present.

2 **a** It is important to distinguish Koreans from Japanese and Chinese because Koreans have had to fight both neighbours in order to retain their independence, and are therefore both proud and bitter about this.

   b There are five main Korean family names: *Kim, Lee* or *Yi, Park* or *Pak, Ch'oe* and *Chong*. One in four Koreans is named *Kim*, and more than half are named *Kim, Lee* or *Park*. Because most Koreans have one of these names, it is easy to learn them, and so recognise their nationality from the name.

3 Education is very highly valued in South Korea, and there is fierce competition for university places. This shows the strength of the Confucian belief that education is the path to success.

4 In order to facilitate business dealings with a Korean, it would be advisable to:

   a arrange for an introduction by an intermediary (for example, an Australian trade representative with connections in Korea);

   b ensure a respectful exchange of cards on first meeting;

   c devote much time at the outset to socialising and to the building up of trust and good personal relationships.

5 The correct answer is **b**. Anger is usually concealed by Koreans, so an open show of anger means that there is a very strong and serious reason for it.

6 The misunderstanding occurred because Koreans do not usually smile at strangers and often avoid speaking to them. They are not used to the superficial friendliness shown to people in general interactions in a culture like the United States.

7 Korean body language which indicated a negative reaction could include tipping the head back, and sucking air through the teeth (making an audible sound).

8 Physical touching is common amongst good male friends in Korea, and such behaviour as touching the thigh of another man, or holding hands

▼

with him, almost certainly means only that the two men are good friends.

9 The two most important foods in Korean cuisine are rice and *kimch'i*.

10 Becoming drunk is generally acceptable in Korean culture because it is thought that people really get to know one another only when drinking heavily together. Drinking and singing are an important part of socialising for Korean males.

Germans

1 Although German culture is essentially individualist, there is still a greater emphasis on the importance of the group than is the case in societies such as the USA or Australia. In an orchestra, the individual performers must each do their best, but they must also consider the joint work of the group if they are to produce good music together.

2 All of the behaviours described in the question would probably be viewed unfavourably by German visitors. Formality is usually valued, and informal friendliness and joking might seem overfamiliar and presumptuous. Germans tend to value precision and expect people to be well informed. Therefore, answers which are vague and general might not be appreciated.

3 a An example of the German tendency not to disturb others is the care taken to telephone others only at certain times.

  b The preference for high hedges and fences around homes is an example of the German emphasis on privacy.

  c The attitude to people crossing against a red light is an example of the German preference for rules and order.

4 An example of German formality is the use of titles and formal terms of address with all but very close friends.

5 Pointing your index finger to your own head is an example of a conversational gesture which is less acceptable to Germans than to Australians. The gesture can be taken as an insult to the other person.

6 Alternative **a** is correct. Requests translated directly from German into English cause problems because a direct translation results in expressions like: 'You will open the door', which can sound like an arrogant order in English, although it would not be so interpreted in German.

7   Germans are eating less meat than used to be the case, and the traditional sausage is less popular. These changes in habit are a result of
health concerns regarding consumption of fat.

8   To suggest that German visitors are interested only in beer and sausages
is a stereotypical view of Germans, many of whom are great travellers
and very cosmopolitan. Would beer and a meat pie keep all Australians
happy when travelling overseas?

9   Time is important to Germans, and not to be wasted. Being kept waiting
by slow, chatty service staff would not be appreciated.

10 The behaviour described is probably not uncommon behaviour amongst
Germans. Cleanliness is highly valued, and the glasses with stains would
be seen as sloppiness and a poor standard of service.

Malaysians

1 a The three main ethnic groups in Malaysia are Malays, Chinese and
Indians.

   b Malays have most of the political power.

2 a The term *bumiputras* ('sons of the soil') refers to the Muslim Malays
and the indigenous groups.

   b Because they have been economically and socially the least advanced
group, the government has been trying to redress the balance in their
favour.

3 The name *Tunku Razaleigh Hitam* would suggest that the guest was a
Malay from Malaysia, and was a male of high status, with a title equivalent to that of a prince.

4 It is quite possible that the unhappy Malay colleague is displeased
because he believes that you have caused him to lose 'face' in public. He
would see this as an unfriendly act and would feel humiliated and hurt.
It would be very difficult for him to act normally towards you.

5 Indians and Malays consider the left hand to be unclean, and the touching of another person's head as taboo.

6 Knives have traditionally been regarded as weapons by Malays, and are
not usually used when eating.

7 A minority of Malays do drink alcohol, arguing that becoming intoxicated is forbidden, but that alcohol itself is not.

8 Malays, Indonesians and Thais prefer long-grained rice, cooked without salt, and served with the grains dry and separate. Koreans and Japanese prefer the short-grained varieties of rice.

9 During the month of Ramadan, all Muslims must fast from sunrise to sunset and abstain from other practices such as smoking and sexual intercourse. At the end of this month they celebrate the *Eid ul-Fitr* festival. This is an important festival to give thanks to Allah and celebrate the end of Ramadan. Since Ramadan occurs in a lunar cycle (and not according to a calendar year), the month occurs at different times from year to year. Strict observance of Ramadan might make it difficult for Muslim employees to work as normal.

10 Malays might find the style of toilet (and the fact that it is in the bathroom) strange. The lack of a hose for washing after defaecating, as well as the style of bath (with no provision for water to drain away from the floor), might also be problematic at first.

Indians

1 India is seen as a tourist market with a big potential because Indian society has a large and growing middle class. If Australia could capture even a small percentage of this potential market, it would represent a very large number of Indian visitors.

2 a Many modern Western ideas are spreading in India because satellite television has been introduced throughout the country.

  b This may lead to Indians becoming more materialistic and individualist because many of the programs come from the United States.

3 a Hinduism is the religion most associated with Indian culture.

  b The hierarchical organisation of Indian society has been shaped by Hinduism because Hindus have traditionally believed that each person belongs to a caste from birth (as a result of their actions in their previous life). These castes form an hierarchy from the highest to the lowest and so make Indians very status conscious.

4 The concept of *dharma* stresses duty, harmony and the interdependence of the group (for example, the extended family). This is important in maintaining the collectivist values which are strong in this society.

5 There is still a widespread preference for sons in Indian culture because a son guarantees the continuation of the family line, and the son performs the last rites after the death of a parent.

6 Communication with English-speaking Indians may be difficult because:

   a some of the grammar and vocabulary is different in Indian English; and

   b some of the accents and intonation patterns (which are influenced by the native languages of Indians) are also different.

7 The conversational gesture of an Indian moving the head from side to side could indicate:

   a that he/she is indicating comprehension of what the speaker is saying; and/or

   b that he/she agrees with what is being said.

8 Indians, Indonesians, Malays and Thais generally share the following beliefs:

   a that the head is sacred and should not be touched;

   b that the soles of the feet (or the soles of shoes) are the lowest, dirtiest part of the body, that they should not be put on furniture, and that they should not touch (or be pointed at) other people; and

   c that the left hand is unclean and, to be polite, one should avoid passing things (such as food) with the left hand.

9 Hindus generally do not eat beef, and many are strict vegetarians. Alcohol is not usually served with meals, and many Indians (especially high-caste Brahmins) may not drink alcohol because they value self-control.

10 Well-off Indians would be used to constant, attentive and very deferential service.

Appendix 1

Notes for teachers

Introducing Cross-Cultural Communication

Some students may question the relevance and importance of studying cross-cultural communication.

It can be useful to begin the course by asking students about their future plans. Usually a number of them will indicate that they hope to work overseas, at least for a short time, at some stage in their careers. This provides an opportunity to point out the nature of the career upon which they are embarking, and to stress the need for an international outlook, even when working in Australia, because of the nature of much of the clientele.

It can then be emphasised that the aim of the course is to provide information that helps develop this international outlook.

Some students may argue that other cultures are converging towards Western standards in the industry and that English has become a 'world language'. Because of the political and economic ascendancy of first Britain, and then the United States, during the last hundred years, this has been true to a considerable extent. However, with the economic growth of other parts of the world, in particular North-East and South-East Asia, the situation is changing.

A number of other arguments about the need for such knowledge have been made in the rationale for cross-cultural training in the *Introduction*. Students could be asked to suggest reasons of their own, and then to check in the *Introduction* to see if they missed any important points.

Case-Studies

Some of the questions in the Questions section are actually mini case-studies (or could be easily adapted to this purpose). In order to raise interest and to test existing knowledge, it might be helpful (before formally studying a particular culture) to take one of these questions, and provide it as a stimulus for class/group discussion.

Alternatively, one of these 'case-study type' questions could be used after studying a particular culture to revise and consolidate knowledge about the specific points involved.

The following questions from the various sections would be the most suitable for this purpose:

Japanese: Questions 3, 6, 10   *Koreans:* Question 6

Thais: Questions 8, 9   *Germans:* Question 10

Americans: Questions 3, 6   *Malaysians* Questions 3, 4

Chinese: Question 6, 7, 9   *Indians:* Questions 7, 10

Indonesians: Questions 2, 3, 6, 8

Role-plays

Role-plays are not always advisable in teaching cross-cultural communication courses as they usually require students to play the part of someone from another culture. This can be difficult, and can result in unintentional stereotyping.

If teachers do want to test students' skills (and their retention of information) by asking them to perform role-plays, it is best to concentrate on content rather than trying to 'act the part' of visitors from particular cultures.

Some of the questions from the Questions section could be adapted to provide material for this purpose. In some instances, 'how not to do it' could be role-played first and then 'how to do it' afterwards. Questions suitable for this purpose include:

Japanese: Questions 3, 4   *Indonesians:* Questions 2, 4

Thais: Questions 6, 7   *South Koreans:* Question 4

Americans: Questions 4, 5, 6   *Germans:* Question 2

Chinese: Questions 6, 7

Facts and Figures

• •

Table 1 International visitors by country of residence (1995-99)

Country of Residence	1995	1996	1997	1998	1999
New Zealand	490 700	609 600	621 100	640 500	660 800
Japan	737 900	766 600	766 000	704 400	662 500
Hong Kong	117 300	137 600	136 600	130 400	127 900
Taiwan	138 300	144 800	138 900	135 100	133 600
Thailand	72 500	80 500	61 800	44 600	55 700
Korea	160 600	216 200	220 500	62 300	100 100
Malaysia	94 400	118 200	125 800	101 800	126 500
Singapore	168 500	185 900	201 300	215 600	234 100
Indonesia	107 600	129 900	138 200	82 600	82 400
China	n.a.	52 300	63 800	73 300	87 500
Other Asia	102 800	74 400	88 700	92 300	101 800
United States	287 600	299 200	309 800	353 200	392 500
Canada	55 000	57 800	60 800	68 100	75 200
United Kingdom	335 400	347 200	387 800	448 400	508 900
Germany	119 800	120 700	124 500	123 500	140 000
Other Europe	258 800	291 400	319 400	343 700	388 500
Other countries	174 700	197 500	209 100	239 200	265 100
TOTAL	3 422 000	3 829 800	3 974 000	3 859 000	4 143 100

Notes:

1. Visitors aged 15 years and over
2. n.a. denotes not available
3. Data for Middle East countries are included in Other Asia in 1989 and 1990 and in Other countries from 1991 onwards.
4. Data for Ireland are included in the United Kingdom from 1989 to 1994 and in Other Europe in 1995.

Source: Bureau of Tourism Research, <www.btr.gov.au>, phone (02) 6213 6940, fax (02) 6213 6983, from whom further information can be obtained.

Table 2 International visitors by main purpose of journey 1995–99

Main Purpose	1995	1996	1997	1998	1999
Holiday	2 047 800	2 290 000	2 302 500	2 094 500	2 295 500
Visiting friends & relatives	631 600	704 100	737 100	788 700	795 300
Business	360 400	391 700	436 100	443 700	440 800
Convention	69 600	98 900	126 800	112 800	118 700
Other	312 500	345 100	371 500	419 200	492 800

Source: Bureau of Tourism Research, <www.btr.gov.au>, phone (02) 6213 6940, fax (02) 6213 6983, from whom further information can be obtained.

Table 3a Expenditure and nights in Australia, 1999

Expenditure and nights	USA and Canada	Japan	Other Asia	NZ	UK	Other Europe	Other	Total
Average expenditure in Australia* ($)	2240	1423	2829	1170	2342	2829	1864	2152
Average expenditure per night* ($)	88	105	90	80	66	74	77	82
Average nights in Australia	25	14	31	15	36	38	24	26
Total nights in Australia (million)	11.8	9.0	33.0	9.7	18.1	20.3	6.5	108.3

* Excludes expenditure on fully inclusive, prepaid package tours and international airfares purchased outside Australia.

Source: Bureau of Tourism Research, <www.btr.gov.au>, phone (02) 6213 6940, fax (02) 6213 6983, from whom further information can be obtained.

Table 3b Expenditure and nights in Australia, 1998

Expenditure and nights	USA and Canada	Japan	Other Asia	NZ	UK	Other Europe	Other	Total
Average expenditure in Australia* ($)	2238	1403	2884	1156	2254	2859	2353	2147
Average expenditure per night* ($)	93	116	93	87	62	73	79	85
Average nights in Australia	24	12	31	13	36	39	30	25
Total nights in Australia (million)	10.1	8.6	29.0	8.5	16.3	18.4	7.1	98

* Excludes expenditure on fully inclusive, prepaid package tours and international airfares purchased outside Australia.

Source: Bureau of Tourism Research, <www.btr.gov.au>, phone (02) 6213 6940, fax (02) 6213 6983, from whom further information can be obtained.

Table 3c Expenditure and nights in Australia, 1997

Expenditure and nights	USA and Canada	Japan	Other Asia	NZ	UK	Other Europe	Other	Total
Average expenditure in Australia* ($)	2116	1343	2554	1200	1937	2330	1946	1953
Average expenditure per night* ($)	87	128	97	82	56	65	73	84
Average nights in Australia	24	11	26	15	35	36	26	23
Total nights in Australia (million)	9	8.1	30.9	9.1	13.5	15.9	5.5	92

* Excludes expenditure on fully inclusive, prepaid package tours and international airfares purchased outside Australia.

Source: Bureau of Tourism Research, <www.btr.gov.au>, phone (02) 6213 6940, fax (02) 6213 6983, from whom further information can be obtained.

Table 4a Nights in states and territories, 1999 (%)

States and territories	USA and Canada	Japan	Other Asia	NZ	UK	Other Europe	Other	Total
New South Wales	33	37	40	30	35	32	38	36
Victoria	19	14	24	19	15	19	15	19
Queensland	27	33	13	37	26	24	27	23
South Australia	5	2	4	2	6	6	3	4
Western Australia	8	10	14	8	13	11	9	11
Tasmania	2	1	2	2	1	1	3	2
Northern Territory	3	2	1	1	4	6	3	3
Australian Capital Territory	2	2	3	1	1	1	3	2
Total	100	100	100	100	100	100	100	100

Source: Bureau of Tourism Research, <www.btr.gov.au>, phone (02) 6213 6940, fax (02) 6213 6983, from whom further information can be obtained.

Table 4b Nights in states and territories, 1998 (%)

States and territories	USA and Canada	Japan	Other Asia	NZ	UK	Other Europe	Other	Total
New South Wales	35	31	38	30	33	33	38	35
Victoria	17	14	29	16	15	16	20	20
Queensland	24	38	12	36	24	23	22	22
South Australia	6	4	3	3	6	6	3	5
Western Australia	8	9	13	11	16	12	8	12
Tasmania	2	1	2	1	1	1	3	2
Northern Territory	6	2	1	2	3	6	2	3
Australian Capital Territory	3	1	3	1	1	2	4	2
Total	100	100	100	100	100	100	100	100

Source: Bureau of Tourism Research, <www.btr.gov.au>, phone (02) 6213 6940, fax (02) 6213 6983, from whom further information can be obtained.

Table 4c Nights in states and territories, 1997 (%)

States and territories	USA and Canada	Japan	Other Asia	NZ	UK	Other Europe	Other	Total
New South Wales	33	31	39	29	34	35	45	35
Victoria	19	9	27	15	15	17	21	20
Queensland	23	41	15	37	23	24	20	23
South Australia	7	3	3	4	6	6	3	4
Western Australia	8	7	12	10	16	8	8	11
Tasmania	1	2	1	3	2	2	1	2
Northern Territory	5	3	1	1	4	7	1	3
Australian Capital Territory	4	3	3	2	1	1	1	2
Total	100	100	100	100	100	100	100	100

Source: Bureau of Tourism Research, <www.btr.gov.au>, phone (02) 6213 6940, fax (02) 6213 6983, from whom further information can be obtained.

Table 5 Top 20 regions visited by international visitors in Australia in 1999

Region visited	Rank	Visitors ('000)	%
Sydney (NSW)	1	2275.6	55.5
Melbourne (Vic.)	2	997.7	24.4
Gold Coast (Qld)	3	875.8	21.4
Tropical North Queensland	4	755.8	18.4
Brisbane (Qld)	5	704.4	17.2
Perth (WA)	6	519.2	12.7
Adelaide (SA)	7	296.8	7.2
Petermann (NT)	8	254.8	6.2
Alice Springs (NT)	9	211.1	5.2
Sunshine Coast (Qld)	10	199.6	4.9
Whitsunday Islands (Qld)	11	197.7	4.8
Northern Rivers (NSW)	12	182.6	4.5
Canberra (ACT)	13	180.7	4.4
Darwin (NT)	14	179.2	4.4
Hervey Bay/Maryborough (Qld)	15	177.9	4.3
Northern (Qld)	16	146.3	3.6
Fitzroy (Qld)	17	121.2	3.0
Western (Vic.)	18	107.7	2.6
Kakadu (NT)	19	98.9	2.4
Hunter (NSW)	20	88.4	2.2
TOTAL VISITORS		**4096.7**	**100**

Notes:
1. Total excludes visitors who did not specify regions visited, and day trippers.
2. The totals of the columns add to more than the total number of visitors because visitors tend to travel to more than one region.

Source: Bureau of Tourism Research, <www.btr.gov.au>, phone (02) 6213 6940, fax (02) 6213 6983, from whom further information can be obtained.

▼

Table 6 Backpacker visitors in Australia 1997–99

	1997	1998	1999
Visitors	306 100	313 900	404 300
Nights in Australia ('000)	20 220	23 708	26 524
Average duration of stay	66	76	66
Total expenditure ($ million)	1 196.3	1 476.5	1 717.0

Note: A backpacker is defined in this table as an international visitor who spent one or more nights in a backpacker hotel or youth hostel during his or her stay in Australia

Source: Bureau of Tourism Research, <www.btr.gov.au>, phone (02) 6213 6940, fax (02) 6213 6983, from whom further information can be obtained.

Table 7 Economic impact of tourism 1997–98

Consumption by visitors	Visitors consumed a total of $58.2 billion in goods and services nationally; 78% ($45.4 billion) was by domestic visitors; 22% ($12.8 billion) was by international visitors.
Exports	Spending by international visitors accounted for 11.2% of total exports.
Gross domestic product (GDP)	Tourism GDP amounted to $25.2 billion, a direct contribution of 4.5% of total GDP.
Employment	Tourism directly employed 513 000 persons, representing 6% of total employment.

Note: Estimates selectively extracted from ABS source. Due to significant changes in the methodology between previous economic estimates and the Australian Tourism Satellite Account, the Bureau of Tourism Research strongly recommends that these data should not be compared with previous economic estimates.

Source: *Australian National Accounts: Tourism Satellite Account 1997–98* (ABS Catalogue No. 5249.0) as posted on website of Bureau of Tourism Research, <www.btr.gov.au>.

Bibliography

• •

Anon. (1991) *Doing Business in Korea*. New York: Ernst & Young International Ltd

Asian Committee on TAFE. Curriculum *Asian Skills Resources for Australia: Introductory and Specialist Japanese Culture Modules*. Queensland Department of Employment, Vocational Training and Employment

Asian Intelligence. Issue #441 July 19,1995 Political & Economic Risk Consultancy Ltd

Australian Tourist Commission (1993) *International Tourism Marketing Manual*. Sydney: Australian Tourist Commission

Axtell, Roger E (1991) *Gestures: the Do's and Taboos of Body Language Around the World*. New York: John Wiley

Barlund, Dean C (1975) 'Communication Styles in Two Cultures: Japan and the United States'. In Kendon, Harris & Keys (eds) *Organisation of Behaviour in Face to Face Interaction*. The Hague: Mouton

Bates, Chris (1995) *Culture Shock: Taiwan*. Singapore: Times Books International

Black, Ian (1993) *Malaysia: Asia-Australia Institute Briefing Paper*. Sydney: University of New South Wales

Bonavia, David (1980) *The Chinese*. New York: Lippincott & Crowell

Brick, Jean (1991) *China: A Handbook in Intercultural Communication*. Sydney: National Centre for English Language Teaching and Research

Brissendon, Rosemary (1996) *South-East Asian Food*. Harmondsworth, Middlesex: Penguin Books

Brown, P & Levinson, S (1987) *Politeness: Some Universals in Language Usage*. Cambridge: Cambridge University Press

Bunge & Shinn (1981) *China: A Country Study*. US Foreign Affairs Studies: The American University

Bureau of Tourism Research (1997) *International Visitor Survey (December Quarter 1996)* Commonwealth of Australia, Canberra

Byrne, Margaret & FitzGerald, Helen (1996) *What Makes You Say That?: Cultural Diversity at Work*. Sydney: SBS Publications

Chang, K C (1977) *Food in Chinese Culture*. New Haven: Yale University Press

Chao, Y R (1976) *Aspects of Chinese Sociolinguistics*. California: Stanford University Press

Choe-Wall, Yang hi, Wall, Ray & Wall, Stephen (1988) *The Korea Fact Book*. Garden City, New York: Doubleday

Chu, Ching-ning (1995) *The Asian Mind Game*. St Ives: Stealth Productions

Clancy, P (1986) 'The Acquisition of Communicative Style in Japanese'. In Schieffelin & Ochs (eds) *Language Socialisation Across Cultures*. Cambridge: Cambridge University Press

Condon & Yousef (1987) 'Out of House and Home'. In Luce & Smith (eds) *Towards Internationalism*. Massachusetts: Newbury Park

Cooper, R & N (1982) *Culture Shock: Thailand*. Singapore: Times Books International

Copeland, L & Grigg, L (1985) *Going International: How to Make Friends and Deal Effectively in the Global Marketplace*. New York: Random House

Dalton, Bill (1995) *Indonesian Handbook*. Chico, California: Moon Publishers

David M. Kennedy Centre for International Studies (Grant Skabelund: Ed.) (1990) *Culturgram for the Nineties*. Utah: Brigham Young University

Draine, Cathie & Hall, Barbara (1995) *Culture Shock: Indonesia*. Singapore: Times Books International

Dunung, Sanjyot (1995) *Doing Business in Asia: The Complete Guide*. New York: Lexington Books

Encarta; 1994 Microsoft Corporation; 1994 Funk & Wagnall's Corporation

Encyclopaedia Britannica 15th Edition; 1943–73; 1973–4; Publishers: William Benton, Helen Hemingway Benton; Chicago/London

Engholm, Christopher (1991) *When Business East Meets Business West: The Guide to Practice and Protocol in the Pacific Rim*. New York: J Wiley

Ferraro, Gary (1990) *The Cultural Dimensions of International Business*. New Jersey: Prentice Hall

Fieg, John (1989) *A Common Core: Thais and Americans*. Yarmouth, Maine: Intercultural Press

Gannon, Martin J & Associates (1994) *Understanding Global Cultures*. California: Sage

Gumperz, J (1982) *Discourse Strategies: Studies in Interactional Sociolinguistics*. Cambridge: Cambridge University Press

Hijirida, Kyoko & Sohn, Ho-min (1986) 'Cross-cultural Patterns of Honorifics and Sociolinguistic Sensitivity to Honorific Variables: Evidence from English, Japanese and Korean'. *Papers in Linguistics* 19 (3)

Hu, W & Grove, C L (1991) *Encountering the Chinese*. Yarnmouth, Maine: Intercultural Press

Hur, Sonia V & Hur, Ben, S (1993) *Culture Shock: Korea*. Singapore: Times Books International

Irwin, H (1996) *Communicating with Asia: Understanding People and Customs*. Sydney: Allen &Unwin

Kataoka, Hiroko & Kusumoto, Tetsuya (1991) *Japanese Cultural Encounters and How to Handle Them*. Illinois: Passport Books

Koyama, Tomoko (1992) Japan: *A Handbook in Intercultural Communication*. Sydney: National Centre for English Language and Research

Lafayette De Mente, Boye (1991) *Behind the Japanese Bow*. Illinois: Passport Books

Lebra, T S & Lebra, W (eds) *Japanese Culture and Behaviour: Selected Readings*. Honolulu: University of Hawaii

Lewer, Simon & Phung, Gia-Nghi (1994) *Asian Connections: A Country by Country Handbook of Asian Culture and Business Practices*. Sydney: Gibsons International Export Development Resources

Little, R & Reed, W (1989) *The Confucian Renaissance*. Annandale, NSW: The Federation Press

MacIntyre, I (1993) *Indonesia: Asia Australia Institute Briefing Papers*. Sydney: University of New South Wales

March, Robert (1996) *Reading the Japanese Mind*. Tokyo: Kodansha International

Matsumoto, Yoshiko (1988) 'Re-examination of the Universality of Face: Politeness Phenomenon in Japan'. In the *Journal of Pragmatics* 12:403–426

Mezger, June (1992) *Bridging the Intercultural Communication Gap: A Guide for TAFE Teachers of International Students*. Hobart: National TAFE Overseas Network

Monroe, Charles (1995) *World Religions: An Introduction*. New York: Prometheus Books

Munan, H (1991) *Culture Shock: Malaysia*. Singapore: Times Books International

Murphy, Rhoads (1992) *A History of Asia*. New York: Harper Collins

Neustupny, J V (1987) *Communicating with the Japanese*. Tokyo: The Japan Times

O'Brien, J & Palmer, M (1993) *State of Religion Atlas*. London: Simon & Schuster

Office of Multicultural Affairs (1995) *Productive Diversity in the Tourism Industry*. Canberra: AGPS

O'Sullivan, Kerry (1994) *Understanding Ways: Communicating Between Cultures*. Sydney: Hale & Iremonger

Pan, Lyn (1987) *The New Chinese Revolution*. London: Hamish Hamilton

Penny, J & Khoo, S E (1996) *Intermarriage: A Study of Migration & Integration*. Canberra: AGPS

Renwick, George (1980) *Interact: Guidelines for Australians and North Americans*. Yarmouth, Maine: Intercultural Press

Samsung (Aust) Pty Ltd (1995) *Korea: Cross-cultural Connections*. Sydney: Samsung

Seagrave, Sterling (1995) *Lords of the Rim: The Invisible Empire of the Overseas Chinese*. London: Bantam Press

Shames, G W & Glover, W G (1989) *World Class Service*. Yarmouth, Maine: Intercultural Press

Sinclair, K & Wong, Po-Yee (1990) *Culture Shock: China*. Singapore: Times Books International

Sohn, Ho-Minh (1983) 'Intercultural Communication in Cognitive Values: Americans and Koreans' In *Language & Linguistics* 9:93–136

Solomon, Charmaine (1976) *The Complete Asian Cookbook*. Sydney: Paul Hamlyn

Sri Owen (1980) *Indonesian Food & Cookery*. London: Prospect Books

Stewart, Edward (1972) *American Cultural Patterns: A Cross-cultural Perspective*. Yarmouth, Maine: Intercultural Press

Victor, David (1992) *International Business Communication*. New York: Harper Collins

Wanning, Esth (1994) *Culture Shock: USA*. Singapore: Times Books International

Wierzbicka, A (1991) *Cross-cultural Pragmatics: The Semantics of Human Interaction*. Berlin: Mouton De Gruyter

Wierzbicka, A (1991) 'Japanese Key Words and Core Cultural Values'. In *Language in Society* 20: 333–83

Young, Linda (1994) *Crosstalk and Culture in Sino-American Communication*. Cambridge: Cambridge University Press

Glossary

Notes

1. All terms listed in this glossary are described with convenient short 'thumbnail' sketches only; they are not meant to be detailed descriptions or definitions, and readers should consult a good dictionary or appropriate textbook for a fuller description or definition.
2. Words in **bold** in the definitions represent terms for which a separate glossary entry exists.
3. Foreign words and technical terms (which are not part of common English) are printed in *italics* at the first mention in definitions in this glossary.

Abba (Aramaic term: 'Father'): form of address used by **Jesus Christ** towards **God**

Abstain/Abstinence (literally: 'to hold from'): to voluntarily refrain from something; to refuse to take something or do something

Accent emphasis in speech; manner of speaking; particular form of pronunciation

Achenese (Indonesian term): **ethnic** group in northern Sumatra

AD (Latin: *Annus Domini:* 'Year of the Lord'): a system of counting the years according to the **Western** style, counting the years beginning with the birth of **Jesus Christ**

Adab (Malaysian term): showing courtesy to all people at all times

Advent the weeks leading up to **Christmas** when some **Christians abstain** from certain foods, drinks and other activities

Affirmative action making decisions and laws which favour a particular disadvantaged group

Affluence/Affluent possession of wealth, money, resources

Afro-Americans American citizens (or residents) of African origin

Agrarian land and farming based; agricultural

Agricultural primary production; cultivating the soil, crops and animals

Aizuchi (Japanese term): conversational response words exchanged frequently between speakers

Allah the name given to **God** by the followers of **Islam**

Altar table or platform used as a focus of **religious** worship

Amalgam mixture, combination; something new created from previously separate things .

Anglican (literally: 'English'): originally the '**Church** of England' in Australia; the second largest **Christian denomination** in Australia with both **Catholic** and **Protestant** traditions amongst its members

Animation (literally: 'life', 'spirit'): showing a lot of activity, spirited

Animist as applied to **religion**: the belief that non-living objects in the natural world have a soul or spirit; a 'nature religion'

Aromatic spicy; fragrant; sweet-smelling

Arranged marriage a marriage organised by people other than the couple to be married

Aryan fair-skinned people originally from central Asia who invaded India in waves from about 1500 BC mixing with the **indigenous Dravidian** population to form the population group which speaks the **Indo-Aryan** languages of northern India such as **Hindi**, **Bengali** and **Gujerati**

Atheist a person who does not believe in any **god**

Autocratic ruled by an absolute (not **democratic**) authority

Avatar (Hindu term): an **incarnation**; the appearance of a **god** in a particular form; the great god **Vishnu**, for example, has various avatars, including **Krishna** and **Rama**

BC (abbreviation for: 'Before **Christ**'): the calendar years as counted in the **Western** system before the birth of **Jesus Christ**

Bahasa Indonesia the national language of Indonesia

Bahasa Malaysia/Bahasa Melayu the national language of Malaysia

Bakmi goreng (Indonesian term): fried noodles

Balinese predominantly **Hindu** people of the island of Bali in Indonesia

Bapak (Indonesian term): honorific title meaning 'father'

Barbarians uncivilised, primitive, violent, cruel people

Bataks (Indonesian term): **ethnic** group of Sumatra

Beating-around-the-bush (Australian idiom): **idiomatic** expression meaning 'indirect'

Beer alcoholic drink made from fermented malt, flavoured with hops

Belum (Indonesian term): 'not yet' (used to avoid a direct negative or refusal)

Bengali the main language of northeastern India and Bangladesh

Bethlehem birth place of **Jesus Christ**, in Palestine south of **Jerusalem**

Bhagavad Gita (Indian term): sacred **Hindu** poem in the *Mahabharata* in which **Krishna** expounds the **religion** of duty *(dharma)*

Bible (also known as Holy Bible): the **sacred text** (holy book) of **Christianity**, composed of the **Old** and **New Testaments**

Biergarten (German term): 'beer garden'; an open-air place for meeting people and drinking **beer**

Bin (Malaysian term): 'son of'

Binti (Malaysian term): 'daughter of'

Bland mild, non-stimulating

Bourbon American whiskey made from a fermented mash of corn, malt and rye

Brahman (Hindu term): the ultimate reality and joy

Brahmin (Hindu term): member of the highest or priestly **caste**

Brandy spiritous drink distilled from **wine** or grapes

Breaking-the-ice (idiomatic expression): 'to become acquainted'

British rule (in India) the British Raj, the period when the British ruled in India (c.1757–1947)

Britons inhabitants of England, Scotland and Wales

Buddha an **Enlightened** One; usually applied, although not exclusively, to **Siddhartha Gautama**

Buddhism **religion** founded by **Siddhartha Gautama (Buddha)** in the 6th century BC who taught that happiness is achieved by destroying desire, attachment and ignorance

Budi (Malaysian term derived from Sanskrit): the showing of courtesy to all people and the encouragement of **harmony** in society

Buffet (literally: a sidetable or sideboard): a buffet-meal is a meal with all available food served on a sidetable from which people make their own selection

Bumiputras (Malaysian term; literally: 'sons of the soil'): **Muslim Malays** and groups native to the area

Burakumin (Japanese term): minority **ethnic** group in Japan

Bureaucracy/bureaucrat the civil service; officials who carry out the functions of government

BYO (abbreviation for: 'bring-your-own'): an arrangement in some Australian restaurants whereby the customer brings their own (unopened) bottle of **wine** to the restaurant

c. (abbreviation of **Latin** *circa*: 'around'): about, approximately (refers to dates)

Cantonese (referring to Canton *(Guangzhou)*, a city in southern China): (1) a Chinese **dialect** spoken in Hong Kong; (2) a **cuisine**

Cappuccino (Italian term; referring to a monk's peaked hood): a type of coffee drink, usually served with steamed milk/cream foam on top

Caste system a system of inherited social divisions within **Hinduism**; *see also Brahmins, Kshatriyas, Vaishayas, Shudras*, **Untouchables**

Catholic (literally: 'universal'): a major division of the **Christian Church** (originally based in western Europe)

CE Christian Era (same as AD)

Ch'aemyon (Korean term): loss of '**face**'

Chao Phya (Thai term): title of high ranking civil servant

Chapati (Indian term): a flat unleavened bread

Characters symbols or letters used in writing words

Christ (literally: 'anointed one'): the **messiah**; applied as a surname to **Jesus Christ**

Christian referring to **Christianity**; a follower of Christianity

Christian era the system of counting the years in **Western** society beginning with the birth of **Jesus Christ** (and adopted for convenience for most international use); *see also* AD and BC

Christianity world-wide **religion** founded by **Jesus Christ**

Christmas festival (25 December each year in the **West**) at which **Christians** celebrate the birth of **Jesus Christ**

Christmas carols hymns with a special emphasis on the themes of the **Christmas** festival

Church the organised **Christian religion**; a building for **Christian** worship

Circuitous going in circles; indirect

Clan an **extended family** or a group of families claiming a common ancestor

Cocktail any alcoholic mixed drink made from spirits, bitters, sugar etc.

Cognac French **brandy**

Collectivist a **culture** or society in which the group (or the State) takes priority over the individual in economic and social matters

Colloquial speech speech using **slang**; conversational speech (sometimes including impolite, non-**deferential** 'taboo' words)

Colonised settled and ruled by people from another country

Colonist settler from another country which has taken over and rules a new country

Colony a country or region ruled by a distant (usually European) country

Commemorate (literally: to remember with): to mention as worthy of rememberance; to remember by some solemnity or **ritual**

Commodity an article of trade, especially a product

Communal shared in common

Communism a political/economic system in which the State (rather than individuals) owns all property, services and the means of production and exchange

Communist referring to **communism**; a believer in communism

Complementary completing; suitable

Compliant co-operative; acting in accordance with the wishes or rules of others

Composure calmness; tranquillity; avoiding expression of emotion

Comprehension understanding

Conformity behaving as others do, or as others would wish

Confucianism one of the major spiritual philosophies of China the influence of which has spread to other Asian countries; a **philosophy** and a system of **ethics** dealing with the individual and society, and personal and family obligations

Confucius also known as **K'ung-tsu**; Chinese philosopher b. 55 BC; founder of **Confucianism**

Connoissuer an excellent judge of art

Consensus general agreement

Conservative people who are characterised by a tendency to keep things unchanged

Constitutional monarchy a system of government in which a king or queen is head of state, but where real power is in the hands of a **democratically** elected government

Contrary opposite; difficult

Core central, basic, important

Coriander an annual **aromatic Eurasian** herb plant used as a seasoning

Corruption immoral behaviour in which favours are given and received in return for personal gain

Cosmopolitan free from national prejudice and limitations; having the varied characteristics of being from all parts of the world

Creed a formal statement of **religious** beliefs

Cross-cultural communication communication and understanding between groups from different **cultures**

Cross the main symbol of **Christianity** commemorating the **crucifixion**, death and **resurrection** of **Jesus Christ**

Crucifixion the death of **Jesus Christ** by suffocation and exhaustion on the **Cross**

Cuisine manner or style of cooking and presenting food in a particular **culture**

Cultural Revolution a movement encouraged by the Chinese **communist** government in the late 60s and early 70s in which old **cultural** habits were actively discouraged, sometimes violently

Culture/cultural the habits, outlook, education, **religion** etc. of a particular group

Dalits (Indian term; literally: 'the **oppressed**'): the name by which the **Untouchables** of India refer to themselves; since Indian independence they have been officially known as *Harijans*

Datin (Malaysian term): wife of a male with the title of **Dato**

Dato (Datu) (Malaysian term): title of male person of high rank

Dayaks (Indonesian term): **ethnic** group of Kalimantan and Sarawak

Deceit/deceitful falsehood; cheating

Decree an authoritative statement of law

Deference/Deferential respect; submission to the opinion or judgment of another

Deity (from **Latin** *deus:* a god): a **god**; a supernatural being to be worshipped

Demeaning lowering dignity; humbling

Democracy/democratic government by the people; a system of government in which power resides with the people

Denomination a division or class of things; used in **religion** to apply to a religious sect or body designated by a particular name

Dharma (Hindu term): the law of right living; the basis of **harmony** and social cohesiveness

Dialect a variation on a common language as spoken by a regional group

Discriminate/discrimination to act in a way which especially affects a particular group in society; usually implying actions which act against the interests of that group (but *see also* **positive discrimination** and **affirmative action**)

Doctrine teaching, learning; the set of beliefs accepted as true by a particular **religion**

Dogma belief or **doctrine** of a **religion**; sometimes used to indicate belief or doctrine which is arrogantly and/or irrationally held

Dowry a gift which a woman brings to her husband at marriage

Dragons mythical fire-breathing reptile-like creatures of importance in Chinese **culture** (*see also* 'mini-dragon')

Dravidians (Indian term): the second largest of the three main **ethnic** or **linguistic** groups making up the Indian population; they tend to live mainly in the south

Easter three-day **Christian** festival held according to a **lunar** calendar in March or April each year celebrating the **crucifixion** and **resurrection** of **Jesus Christ**

Echelon one of a series of levels

Egalitarian equal for all people

Eid ul-Fitr (Islamic term): an important three-day **Muslim** festival held to give thanks to **Allah** and celebrate the end of **Ramadan**

Empathy feeling as someone else does; imagining yourself to be in the other person's position

Encik (Malaysian term): form of address meaning 'Mr'

Enlighten/Enlightenment (literally: 'to give light to'): to receive knowledge, wisdom, understanding; a state of great knowledge, understanding, wisdom

Enryo (Japanese term): concept of personal behaviour best described as 'reserve'

Entrée (literally French: 'entrance'): the first course of a meal; (but note: used in American **idiom** to mean the main course)

Epic (from the Greek word *epos:* a narrative poem): a literary work (originally a narrative poem) about a nation's history and heroes

Equality of opportunity the idea that everyone should have the same chance (or opportunity) to succeed in life

Equality of outcome the idea that everyone should end up with the same success in life (rather than merely having the same opportunity to succeed)

Ethic/ethics (from the Greek word for 'character'): morality; that which is proper; in accordance with accepted rules of conduct

Ethnic (literally: 'heathen'): originally a term used to describe gentile (non-**Jewish**) nationalities or **religions**; in modern use, a description of a particular **cultural** group or nationality

Ethnically homogenous populated by people from the same racial group

Etiquette accepted rules of polite behaviour

Eucharist the central ceremony of **Christian** worship (also called 'Mass', 'Lord's Supper' and 'Holy Communion') commemorating the last supper of **Jesus** and his followers

Eurasian of mixed European and Asian ancestry

Explicit open, obvious, not hidden

Extended family family members apart from parents and children (including aunts, uncles, nephews, nieces, cousins, grandparents etc.)

Extroverted outgoing, open, confident

Face as in 'losing face' and 'saving face': losing or retaining personal prestige

Fad enthusiastic (but temporary) interest in something

Fast/fasting going without food and drink; (note: the English term 'breakfast' is derived from the 'breaking' of the overnight fast)

Fatalism the idea that a person's fate is pre-determined, or at least is beyond a person's ability to control through the exercise of free will

Feng shui Chinese term: the orientation of a building and its ability to harbour good-luck spirits and deter bad-luck spirits

Filial piety the obligation of children to show dutiful respect and care for parents

Fluent flowing, smooth, without hesitation

Frau (German term): title for a married woman; Mrs

Fraulein (German term): title for an unmarried woman; Miss; (now no longer in common use)

Frugality being careful, economical, sparing in use of food, goods, money

Fundamentalism absolute faith in the accuracy of the **sacred text** (holy book) or **creed** of a **religion**; the religious attitude of a person who strictly follows a religion in all legal aspects

Fusion joining together

Ghee (originally a term from **Hindi**): butter which has been clarified (that is, salt, water and meat juices removed to make pure)

Gin alcoholic spirit distilled from grain or malt

Ginseng (in Chinese: *jen shen)*: a plant found in northern China, eastern USA and elswhere, especially valued for the root which has medicinal uses

Glutinous sticky, gluey

God 1. (as in 'a god'): supernatural **deity** worthy of worship; 2. (as in 'the God'): the single ultimate reality of all existence as acknowledged by **Christianity, Islam** and **Judaism**

Gotong-royang (Indonesian term): mutual assistance

Gourmet a **connoisseur** of food and drink

Grammar the rules governing the use and structure of a language

Guan xi (Chinese term): 'to concern, to relate, to make connections, to make relationships'; giving and returning of favours, important for getting things done

Gujerati (Indian term): an important western Indian language

Guru (Indian term adopted into English): a spiritual teacher

Hadiah (Malaysian term): giving gifts

Hadith (Islamic term): a **sacred text** of **Islam**; collection of sayings and events in the life of **Muhammad**

Hajji (Islamic term): male person who has made the pilgrimage (*hajj*) to **Mecca**

Hajj (Islamic term): one of the pillars of **Islam**; the pilgrimage to **Mecca** which every good **Muslim** is supposed to make at least once in a lifetime; *see also haji* and *hajjah*

Hajjah (Islamic term): female person who has made the pilgrimage (*hajj*) to **Mecca**

Hakka a Chinese **dialect**

Halal (Islamic term from the Arabic word for 'lawful'): meat slaughtered according to **Islamic ritual** requirements

Halus (Indonesian term): refined, fine, polite

Han Chinese the dominant **ethnic** population group of mainland China.

Hangul (Korean term): the **phonetic alphabet** of the Korean language

Haragei (Japanese term: literally: 'belly language'): refers to the **intuitive** power to know what another person is thinking, by reading non-verbal cues

Haram (Islamic term): forbidden

Harijans (Indian term: 'God's people'): polite name for the **Untouchables**, popularised by **Mahatma Gandhi**; Hari is one of the names of **Vishnu**

Harmony things working together pleasantly for a desirable outcome

Herr (German term): title for an adult male; Mr

Hierarchical a social system based on definite ordered levels of status and power

Hinayana (Buddhist term; 'Lesser Vehicle'): one of the two main schools of **Buddhism**; also known as **Theravada** ('Way of the Elders'); *see also* **Mayahana**

Hindi (Indian term): a northern and central Indian language, the official national language of India and the most commonly spoken Indian language

Hindu referring to **Hinduism**; a follower of **Hinduism**

Hinduism Indian **religion**; probably the oldest of the main world religions; a code of conduct and a body of beliefs

Hindus originally: ancient civilisation of the Indus River valley (modern-day Pakistan); now usually taken to refer to the followers of **Hinduism**; the majority of the population of India

Hispanics American citizens (or residents) of Spanish or Latin American origin

Hokkien Chinese **dialect**

Homogeneous having all the parts very similar to one another

Honeymooners a couple, just married, on a holiday together

Honne (Japanese term): the truth; the substance of a matter

Hot Cross Bun a type of sweet bread roll shared by **Christians** at **Easter** to **commemorate** the **crucifixion** of **Jesus Christ**

Humiliation embarrassment to the point of complete loss of dignity

Ibu (Indonesian term): honorific title meaning 'mother'

Ideology an organised system of beliefs which governs attitudes to most other matters

Idiom/idiomatic expression form of expression especially found in a particular language, sometimes involving non-literal meaning for words; for example: the American use of the term '**entrée**'

▼

Idiosyncrasies particular individual habits or peculiarities

Immigrants persons who have arrived to settle from another country

In-groups members of a group sharing certain characteristics (for example: family groups, **cultural** groups)

Incarnation (literally: 'to be made flesh'): embodiment; loosely used to refer to 'a life'

Indigenous born in (or native to) a particular land

Indo-Aryans the largest of the three main **ethnic** or **linguistic** groups making up the Indian population; they tend to live mainly in the north of the country and speak Indo-**Aryan** languages such as **Hindi**

Industrialised an economy characterised by factories and industries as opposed to one dependent on **agricultural** products

Integrated to have become part of the whole, or one

Intercommunal between communities

Intercultural a situation or attitude characterised by an awareness of different **cultural** traditions; *see also* **monocultural**

Intermarriage marriage between members of different **ethnic**, **cultural** or **caste** groups

Intermediary a 'middle-man'; one who acts between two parties to carry out business

Intonation patterns ways of pronouncing words; emphasis on words and **syllables**

Intuitive knowing or sensing something immediately without any reasoning process

Islam (literally: 'submission to the will of **Allah**'): a major world **religion** based on the teachings of Allah as conveyed by the **prophet Muhammad**

Jai rohn (Thai term; literally: 'hot heart'): being open about feelings, especially displeasure

Jai yen (Thai term; literally: 'cool heart'): concealing feelings; avoidance of unpleasantness

Jainism a **Hindu** sect founded at much the same time as **Buddhism** (about 500 BC) and sharing many of its ideas; Jains are now found mostly in western India and are very strict **vegetarians**

Jamkaret (Indonesian term; literally: 'rubber time'): expression used to explain lateness

Jangan memalukan (Indonesian term): not to bring shame to oneself and others

Jati (Indian term): a sub-**caste** within one of the traditional **Hindu** orders or *varnas*; for most practical purposes, the *jatis* are the castes into which Hindu society is divided

Javanese the largest **ethnic** group in Indonesia; the people of the island of Java

Jerusalem holy city in modern day Israel (Palestine) revered by **Christians, Jews** and **Muslims**

Jesus (also called Jesus **Christ**; literally: 'Jesus the **Messiah**'): **Jewish prophet**; the founder of **Christianity**

Jew/Jewish (derived from the **patriarch** Judah and his tribe): a person of Hebrew descent; a believer in **Judaism**

Jong Guo (Chinese term; literally: 'the central country'): name for the Chinese homeland

Judaism the **religion** of the Jewish people

Kah jok (Korean term; literally: 'family'): refers to **extended family** of grandparents, their sons, the sons' wives and the sons' children

Kannada (Indian term): a language of southern India

Karma in **Buddhism** and **Hinduism**, the consequence of all a person thinks and does which decides his/her destiny in the next **incarnation**

Kasar (Indonesian term): coarse, unmannered

Khun (Thai term): equivalent of 'Mr' or 'Mrs' or 'Miss'

Kibun (Korean term; no exact equivalent in English): refers to a person's 'mood or current state of mind'; related to '**face**'

Kidding (English language **slang**): friendly teasing; making fun of someone in a friendly way

Kimch'i (Korean term): a popular spicy pickled dish; chief ingredients of which are Korean cabbage and radish, together with various spices

Koran (Qur'an) the **sacred text** (holy book) of **Islam**

Krengja (Thai term): respect or consideration

Krengklua (Thai term; literally: 'fear'): a breakdown of *krengja*

Krishna (Hindu term): a very important god; an *avatar* of **Vishnu** who explains the concept of **dharma** in the *Bhagavad Gita*

Kshatriyas (Hindu term): the second of the four **varnas** or **castes** into which **Hindu** society was theoretically divided; originally warriors and administrators

K'ung-tsu Chinese philosopher also known as **Confucius** (*see also* **Confucianism**)

Lalap (Indonesian term): raw vegetables

Lao-tzu Chinese **sage** who founded **Taoism**

Last rites a **religious** ceremony performed for a person who is dying

Latin the language of the ancient Roman Empire, of learning until the eighteenth century, and of the Roman **Catholic Church** until the 1960s

Lent the weeks leading up to **Easter**, when some **Christians abstain** from certain foods and drinks, and other activities

Li (Confucian concept): courtesy, politeness, respect

Lineage a list of ancestors; a pedigree

Linguistic referring to language and speech

Literacy ability to read and write

Luang (Thai term): title of high ranking civil servant

Lunar referring to the moon and its cycle around the earth

Lutheran a member of the Lutheran **Church**, a **Protestant Christian denomination** based on the teachings of Martin Luther (1483–1546)

Madhyamika (Buddhist term): a 'middle view' or 'path' opposed equally to the extremes of denial and indulgence

Mahabharata (Hindu term) one of the great **Hindu epics** which contains the Hindu **sacred text** known as the **Bhagavad Gita**

Mahatma (Indian term; literally 'great soul'): name given to some Hindu spiritual or moral leaders, for example Mahatma Gandhi (1869–1948), the leader of the campaign for Indian independence

Mahayana (Buddhist term; literally: 'the Great Vehicle'): one of the two major branches of **Buddhism** (the other being *Theravada* or **Hinayana**)

Makruh (Islamic term): permitted, but not encouraged

Malay the largest **ethnic** group in Indonesia and Malaysia; the language of the Malay people

Malayalam (Indian term): a **Dravidian** language of southern India

Malu (Indonesian term): loss of '**face**'; shame

Mandarin the national language of China

Marinated food (usually meat) soaked in spices or flavourings

Marriage dowry the gift a woman brings to her husband at marriage

Martini a **cocktail** of gin and **vodka** or dry **vermouth**

Material comfort money, wealth, possessions

Material success success in life as measured by wealth and possessions

Mateship friendship; mutual help (a term especially used in Australia)

Matriarchal based on the mother as ruler or head of the family

Mecca the holiest city of **Islam**; birthplace of **Muhammad**, in what is now Saudi Arabia

Meditation devotional thought, contemplation or prayer, often in a trancelike state

▼

Meishi (Japanese term): business cards

Melting pot (a **metaphorical** term): a society in which a number of **cultures** have come together to form a new mixed culture

Mentorship a relationship in which an older, more experienced person gives advice and assists with learning and training

Messiah (Aramaic and Hebrew term; literally: 'the anointed one'): long awaited deliverer (or saviour) of the Jewish people; believed by **Christians** to be **Jesus Christ**

Metaphor application of a descriptive term or name to something to which it can be imaginatively (but not literally) applied; for example: '**melting pot**'

Middle East the countries of the eastern Mediterranean including Israel and the Arab nations

Minangkabau (Indonesian term): **Muslim ethnic** group of Sumatra who have a **matriarchical** society in which the women of the family own the property

Mini-dragons (idiomatic term): the fast-developing economies of Taiwan, Hong Kong, Singapore and South Korea

Moksha (Hindu term): to release from the cycle of birth and death by merging with *Brahman*

Mom Chao (Thai term; usually abbreviated to M.C.): child of **Phra Ong Chao**

Mom Rajawong (Thai term; usually abbreviated to M.R.): child of **Mom Chao**

Monarchy a system of government in which a king or queen is head of state (*see also* **constitutional monarchy**)

Monocultural a situation or attitude characterised by a lack of awareness of **cultural** traditions different from one's own; *see also* **intercultural**

Mosaic Laws the basic laws of **Judaism** as laid down by **Moses**

Moses important liberator and lawgiver of the **Jewish** people

Mosque a **Muslim** place of worship

Muhammad (various spellings in English): **prophet** and teacher in Arabia (c.570–632 CE); founder of **Islam**

Multi-ethnic population a population consisting of a number of **ethnic** groups

Muslim referring to **Islam**; a follower of **Islam**

Musyawarah mufakat (Indonesian term): decision by **consensus**

Nam pla (Thai term): fish sauce

Namaste (Indian term): a palms-together greeting used at any time of day, both on meeting and departing

Nasi (Indonesian term): means both 'rice' and 'meal'

Nasi goreng (Indonesian term): rice fried with shrimp, meat and sauces

Negligent lacking proper duty of care

Nepotism the promotion of family members in an organisation, rather than the best person for the job

New Testament the second part of the **Christian Bible** recording the life (and reflections upon the life) of **Jesus Christ** and his followers

Ngan (Thai term): 1. 'work'; 2. also translates as 'play'

Nirvana (Buddhist term): ideal state of happiness or bliss free of all material and earthly desires

Nit-pickers (English **slang** term): people who are especially concerned about detail to an extreme degree

Norm the usual way of behaving (shortened form of 'normal')

Nuclear family parents and immediate children

Nunchi (Korean term): the ability to sense another's *kibun*

Obligatory something which is required; involuntary

Obscene indecent, rude, especially grossly so

Old Testament the **sacred texts** (holy books) of **Judaism**; the first part of the **Christian Bible**

Omoiyari (Japanese term): empathy; feeling as someone else feels

Oppressed being strictly and unfairly controlled by a stronger power

Orthodox (literally: 'right-believing'): (1) a major division of **Christianity**, originally centred on eastern Europe/western Asia; (2) a strict follower of the traditions of a **religion** (for example, 'an orthodox Jew', 'an orthodox **Brahmin**', etc.)

Pancasila (Indonesian term meaning 'five principles'): a State-sponsored **philosophy** to guide the developing sense of unity and nationhood

Paternal referring to a father; fatherly or father-like

Patriarch/Patriarchal based on the father as ruler or head of the family

Perk shortened **slang** form of **perquisite** *(see below)*

Perquisite additional income or gift associated with a particular position or job

Pervasive extending right through; spreading throughout

Philosophy the belief systems and truths which people bring to their practical affairs

Phonetic alphabet an alphabet in which each letter has only one sound, no matter which word it is in

Phra Ong Chao (Thai term; usually abbreviated as P.O.C.): grandchild of King

Phya (Thai term): title of high ranking civil servant

Point A to point Z (English **colloquial** expression): beginning at the first point and proceeding logically through until the end

Pope (from Italian 'Il Papa': 'father'): the Bishop of Rome, the head of the Roman **Catholic (Christian) Church**

Positive discrimination acts which especially assist a particular group in society

Pra (Thai term): title of high ranking civil servant

Prathet Thai (Thai term; literally: 'land of the free'): name for Thailand

Pristine fresh; as new; unpolluted

Proficiency skill, ability

Profound (literally: deep, reaching to the bottom): very learned; intellectually deep

Prophet spokesman or interpreter of the will of **God**

Propriety that which is proper; **conformity** with requirement, rule or principle

Propitious favourable; appropriate; gracious; advantageous

Protectorate a weaker state controlled and protected by a stronger state

Protestant work ethic a view of life derived from **Protestantism** emphasising hard work and personal responsibility for one's success in life

Protestant referring to **Protestantism**; a follower of Protestantism *(see below)*

Protestantism a major division of **Christianity** which split from the (Roman) **Catholic Church** in the 16th century, and which emphasises individual relationship with **God**

Puan Sri (Malaysian term): wife of male with the title of 'Tan Sri'

Puan (Malaysian term): form of address meaning 'Mrs'

Punctuality the habit of being on time for appointments, events etc.

Purdah a screen which hides women from the sight of men or strangers; a system under which women stay inside the house or are hidden from men by veils

Rama (Hindu term): a **Hindu god**, an **avatar** of **Vishnu**, hero of the *Ramayana* epic

Ramadan (Islamic term): the ninth month of the **Muslim lunar** year during which Muslims do not take food between dawn and sunset, do not smoke and do not have sexual relations

Ramayana (Hindu term): one of the great **Hindu epics**, the hero of which is **Rama**

Recalcitrant not **compliant**, not co-operative

Refinement politeness, **culture**; manners, courtesy

Reincarnation the belief that people die and return to life, using different bodies in different lives or **incarnations**

Religion/Religious relating to a belief system about ultimate realities which directs behaviour towards an ideal life

Resurrection term used to describe the life after death of **Jesus Christ**; an important part of **Christian** faith

Retrenched 'sacked', dismissed from one's employment or job

Reunification (literally: 'made one again'): the union of West and East Germany on 3 October 1990 following the collapse of the **communist** state in East Germany

Rituals formal procedures or acts carried out (usually, but not exclusively, in a **religious** ceremony)

Rukun (Malaysian term): acting in ways that encourage harmony in the family, the community and the whole society.

Run amok (English expression borrowed from **Bahasa Malaysia**; *amok:* 'frenzied'): to behave in a violent, riotous, uncontrolled manner

Rural countryside (as opposed to city areas)

Sacred text a book or books of special significiance to particular **religions**

Sage wise person

Saké Japanese fermented liquor made from rice

Salaam (Islamic greeting): 'peace' (be upon you)

Salutation greeting

Salwar-kameez (Indian term): garments: a long shirt over baggy trousers gathered at the ankle

Sambal (Indonesian term): hot sauce made from chilli peppers

San (Japanese term): formal title (roughly equivalent to 'Mr' or 'Mrs')

Sanskrit the literary language of ancient India in which the sacred texts of **Hinduism** are written; **Hindi**, the most important modern Indian language, is derived mainly from Sanskrit and uses the Sanskrit script

Sanuk (Thai term): 'the joy of living'; 'a good time'

Sappari (Japanese term): neat, clean, honest

Sardonic sneering, sarcastic, ironic

Sari the common dress of most Indian women consisting of a long piece of cloth wrapped around the waist and draped over the shoulder or head

Sassuru (Japanese term): the ability to anticipate another person's message **intuitively**

Saté (Indonesian term): roasted chunks of meat or chicken served with peanut sauce

Sawadee (Thai term): common word of salutation; similar to the Hawaiian *aloha*

Scotch shortened form of 'Scotch whisky' (note that **whisky** is often referred to simply as 'Scotch' in Asia)

Secular not **religious**

Selamat (Islamic greeting in Malaysia and Indonesia): 'blessings' or 'peace'; *see also* **salaam**

Semangat (Indonesian term): 'life force'

Send up (English **slang**): to mock; to make fun of; to satirise

She'll do; she'll be right mate (Australian **slang**): 'things will be all right'

Sherbet a fruit-flavoured soft drink made, for example, of water flavoured with lemon juice and sugar

Shi'ite or Shia (Islamic term): one of the two major sects of **Islam** (the other being **Sunni**)

Shintoism (derived from Japanese for 'the way of the gods'): the original **religion** of Japan (which is the only country in which this religion is followed)

Shiva (Hindu term): a very important **god**; a god of fertility and destruction

Shrine a place where devotions are offered to a **deity** or saint; a temple; a **church**

Shudras (Hindu term): the fourth of the four **varnas** or **castes** into which **Hindu** society was theoretically divided; the peasants and craftsmen

Siddhartha Gautama (c. 560–480 BC) Indian prince; founder of **Buddhism**

Sikhs a **religious** sect established in the Punjab region of northern India by **Guru** Nanak in the early 16th century; all male Sikhs carry the name Singh; all females carry the name Kaur; Sikhs can easily be recognised because the men are bearded and wear turbans

Sino-Thais Chinese-Thais

Slang informal language; not standard speech; **colloquial** speech

Sloppy lacking care, inattentive to detail

Soto encounters (Japanese term): encounters with outsiders

Sovereignty rule, authority

Spotless absolutely clean, unsoiled, without a mark

Staple having a chief place amongst the things produced or consumed in a region

Status quo (derived from a longer Latin phrase): the existing state of things

Stereotype (literally: 'solid print'): something stated repeatedly until it is accepted as truth even if it is not strictly accurate

Stratification to be arranged in a series of layers or levels

Sundanese (Indonesian term): strict, **fundamentalist Islamic** group in western **Java**

Sunni (Islamic term): one of the two major sects of **Islam** (the other being **Shia**)

Suntory (Japanese term): a popular Japanese brand of **whisky** and other alcoholic drinks

Superior a boss, a senior person

Switch-off (English **idiom**): to lose interest, to become bored

Syllables parts of words

Symphonic orchestra a large musical group assembled to perform a **symphony** together

Symphony (literally: 'sounding together'): a complex musical composition usually consisting of four contrasting movements

Synchronicity working at the same time

Taboo (originally a Tongan word, now incorporated into English): forbidden

Tactful delicate, careful (in what is done and said)

Tamil an **ethnic** group of southern India and northern Sri Lanka; the most important southern Indian language

Tan-sri (Malaysian term): title of male person of high rank, ranking below **Tan**

Tan (Malaysian term): title of male person of high rank

Tao (Dao) central concept in **Confucianism** where individuals strive to relate their actions and lives to eternal truths, **virtue**, and social **harmony**

Taoism (Daoism) one of the major spiritual philosophies (or 'ways') of China, also influential in Japan, Korea and Vietnam

Tatemae (Japanese term): the official or public position on a matter

Telugu (Indian term): a **Dravidian** language of southern India

Tenets (literally: 'held') opinions, beliefs held as true

Tengku (Malaysian term): a title roughly equivalent to 'Princess'

Theravada (Buddhist term): one of the two major divisions of **Buddhism** (the other being *Mahayana*), as practised in Thailand, which holds the belief that only ordained monks and nuns can achieve **nirvana**; (note: the *Theravada* division of Buddhism is also known as *Hinayana*)

Third World the underdeveloped countries of Asia, Africa and Latin America

Tidak apa (Malay term): a feeling of indifference to the ordinary tasks of daily life; **fatalism**

Tika (Indian term): a dot in the middle of the forehead of Indian women (and some men); it can have **religious** significance, indicating **caste** or marital status, but now it is often merely a part of women's fashion

Tip, tipping small amount of cash given to a waiter or porter in thanks for service (difficulties arise if there is confusion as to whether this is voluntary or expected)

Toh Puan (Malaysian term): wife of male with title of **Tan**

Transitory temporary, not lasting

Tunku (Malaysian term): a title roughly equivalent to 'Prince'

Uchi interactions (Japanese term): interactions with fellow members of 'in-groups'

Uncouth rude, ill-mannered, offensive

Unfilial not doing one's duty as a son or daughter

Unpalatable (literally: unpleasant taste): unacceptable; disliked

Untouchables the lowest or least privileged group in **Hindu** society (so-called because high-**caste Hindus** believed that touching an Untouchable would make the higher caste impure); since Indian independence officially called *Harijans*, but who now prefer to be called *Dalits*

Urban/Urbanised related to cities or towns (as opposed to the countryside)

Vaishyas (Hindu term): the third of the four **varnas** or **castes** into which **Hindu** society was theoretically divided; the farmers, artisans and business classes

Varnas (Hindu term; literally: 'colours'): the four orders or **castes** into which **Hindu** society was divided according to the ancient Hindu texts; *see also* **jati**

Vedas (Hindu term): the most ancient **sacred texts** of **Hinduism**

Vegetarian a person who does not eat meat products

Veneration worship; reverential treatment

Vermouth white **wine** flavoured with **aromatic** herbs

Vices evil doing; wrong actions

Vilify to speak evil of

Virtuous/virtue good, moral, honourable, right-living

Vishnu (Hindu term): one of the principal **gods** of **Hinduism**, most commonly worshipped nowadays in the forms of the popular **avatars Krishna** and **Rama**

Vodka alcoholic spirit (especially Russian) distilled from rye

Wai (Thai term): placing the hands together at the chest and lowering the head in greeting

Wayang (Indonesian term; literally 'shadow'): **Javanese** puppet drama dating from the 10th century CE depicting scenes from **Hindu epics**

Western/Western societies/Western world relating to the societies of Europe, North America, Australia and New Zealand

Whisky a spiritous alcoholic drink distilled from malted barley

Wine alcoholic drink prepared by fermentation of grape juice

Yang guidz (Chinese term; literally: 'foreign devils'): a Chinese term for foreigners

Yang (Confucian/Taoist term): refers to 'gentle, **intuitive**, passive, female'

Yin (Confucian/Taoist term): refers to: 'strong, intellectual, assertive, male'

Zen (or *Ch'an*): **Buddhist** school that developed in China, and later in Japan, as the result of a **fusion** between the **Mahayana** form of **Buddhism** originating in India and the Chinese philosophy of **Taoism**

Index

Notes

1. **bold** indicates main entry
2. *italics* indicates illustration